SOCIAL PERSPECTIVES IN THE 21ST CENTURY

UNDERSTANDING POWER AND EMOTION

AN INTRODUCTION

SOCIAL PERSPECTIVES IN THE 21ST CENTURY

JASON L. POWELL - SERIES EDITOR
UNIVERSITY OF LIVERPOOL, U.K.

Foucault: Issues and Legacy
Jason L. Powell
2012. ISBN: 978-1-62257-539-8

Feminism
Jason L. Powell
2012. ISBN: 978-1-62257-540-4

Baudrillard and Postmodernism
Jason L. Powell
2012. ISBN: 978-1-62257-541-1

Habermas
Jason L. Powell
2012. ISBN: 978-1-62257-542-8

**Understanding Foucault:
For Beginners**
Jason L. Powell
2013. ISBN: 978-1-62417-195-6

**Understanding Power and Emption:
An Introduction**
Jason L. Powell
2013. ISBN: 978-1-62417-200-7

**Understanding Risk and Trust:
A Short Conceptual Examination**
Jason L. Powell
2013. ISBN: 978-1-62417-202-1

SOCIAL PERSPECTIVES IN THE 21ST CENTURY

UNDERSTANDING POWER AND EMOTION

AN INTRODUCTION

JASON L. POWELL

New York

For permission to use material from this book please contact us:
Telephone 631-231-7269; Fax 631-231-8175
Web Site: http://www.novapublishers.com

NOTICE TO THE READER

The Publisher has taken reasonable care in the preparation of this book, but makes no expressed or implied warranty of any kind and assumes no responsibility for any errors or omissions. No liability is assumed for incidental or consequential damages in connection with or arising out of information contained in this book. The Publisher shall not be liable for any special, consequential, or exemplary damages resulting, in whole or in part, from the readers' use of, or reliance upon, this material. Any parts of this book based on government reports are so indicated and copyright is claimed for those parts to the extent applicable to compilations of such works.

Independent verification should be sought for any data, advice or recommendations contained in this book. In addition, no responsibility is assumed by the publisher for any injury and/or damage to persons or property arising from any methods, products, instructions, ideas or otherwise contained in this publication.

This publication is designed to provide accurate and authoritative information with regard to the subject matter covered herein. It is sold with the clear understanding that the Publisher is not engaged in rendering legal or any other professional services. If legal or any other expert assistance is required, the services of a competent person should be sought. FROM A DECLARATION OF PARTICIPANTS JOINTLY ADOPTED BY A COMMITTEE OF THE AMERICAN BAR ASSOCIATION AND A COMMITTEE OF PUBLISHERS.

Additional color graphics may be available in the e-book version of this book.

Library of Congress Cataloging-in-Publication Data
Understanding power and emotion : an introduction / Jason L. Powell (University of Central Lancashire, UK).
     pages cm
 Includes bibliographical references and index.
 ISBN: 978-1-62417-200-7 (pbk.)
 1. Power (Social sciences) 2. Emotions. I. Powell, Jason L., 1971-
HN49.P6.U53 2013
303.3--dc23
                          2012040822

Published by Nova Science Publishers, Inc. ✝ *New York*

CONTENTS

PREFACE

This book explores the concept of power and emotion. The book begins by examining the conceptual problems and issues associated with theorizing power drawing from classical, modern and contemporary social science perspectives. It moves to assess the issues of power elites and relationship to how society is governed. To further examine, this attention moves to global power and the impact that has on power, politics and decision making processes. The book explores power and communication drawing from critical theory and the possibilities for social change. Finally, the book explores the power of emotion and its differential and contested understanding requires a new appropriation of linking what C. Wright Mills calls 'personal troubles' and 'public issues'.

Chapter 1

INTRODUCTION

This text covers an introduction to key theoretical issues in understanding power and emotion in social theory drawing on the lessons learnt from C Wright Mills' important work on the interplay between individuals biographies and the social structures that shape, constrain and facilitate them. In "The Sociological Imagination" (1959), Mills powerfully illustrates that the sociologist seeks, first, to understand the relationship of personal troubles and public issues and the intersection of biography and history; then, these polarities, and the ways in which sociologists address them, define the central problems of social theory in modernity. Mills further argues that the role of the sociologist is to reveal the connections between what is going on in the world and what may be happening within ourselves—in other words, "to grasp history and biography and the relations between the two within society." Mills believed that sociologists develop a quality of mind that enables them to show individuals how their own private troubles may be linked to features of the "public world" of modern society. Mills suggested that the promise and responsibility of the discipline of sociology lie in giving individuals the conceptual tools to make distinctions between "personal troubles" and "public issues." Social theorists can make this distinction if they have a social context and a sense of history from which to understand and situate personal experiences such as understanding power and emotion.

The ability to shift perspectives, to analyze an experience or an issue from many levels of analysis and to see the intersection of these levels and mutual influence, is the heart of the sociological imagination. If we develop a new understanding of our own attitudes about because we learn about how societies construct meanings of power and emotional experiences, then we will have experienced the "sociological imagination." As Mills (1959, 5) points out: "No social study that does not come back to the problem of biography, of history and of their intersections within a society has completed its intellectual journey."

With these "tools for thinking," Mills focuses our attention on the broad social structures that shape our personal stories. Equipped with this understanding, we can go on to understand how "by the fact of our living, we contribute, however minutely, to the shaping of our society and the course of history, even as we are made by society and its historical push" (Mills 1959, 4). Accordingly, we need to be aware of how our personal knowledge is shaped by ourselves and by society as a whole.

Drawing from this definition and process of the "sociological imagination" and the interplay between social context and individuals; this text explores some of the taken-for-granted assumptions that are socially con- structed by society and filter through to shape personal attitudes about power, communication and emotion in everyday life.

The text focuses on the following. Chapter two explores the concept and contestation of power drawing on different theoretical approaches. Chapter three explores the importance of C Weight Mills's work on power elites. Chapter four explores the issue of global power and implications. Chapter five picks up the key issue of communication action and its relationship to power. The final chapter attempts to explore emotion and how its different layers provide important conceptual and theoretical questions for social theorists to ponder.

Chapter 2

WHAT IS POWER?

Power is an "essentially contested and complex term" (Lukes 1974: 7) that cuts right across social science disciplines. The literature on power is marked by a deep disagreement over the basic definition of power. Some theorists define power as getting someone else to do what you want them to do (power over), whereas others define it more broadly as an ability or a capacity to act (power to). Thomas Hobbes's (1985 [1641]: 150) definition of power as a person's "present means ... to obtain some future apparent Good" is a classic example of this understanding of power, as is Hannah Arendt's definition of power as "the human ability not just to act but to act in concert" (1970: 44). Conversely, Michel Foucault (1977) suggests that power itself is "relational" in that whilst one social actor may exercise power with other individuals, we also need to be aware that all other individuals have "power" in their social relationship that can be expressed through "resistance".

The historical emergence of sociological discussions of power has been crystallized in the work of Max Weber. In Max Weber's famous work, *Economy and Society: An Outline of Interpretive Sociology*, he clarifies his typology of power. Weber highlights the distinction between coercive power and power based on various types of authority: charismatic, traditional, and legal rational. People obey charismatic leaders because of the personal qualities of the person doing the telling. Well-known charismatic figures include Jesus Christ and Hitler. However, charismatic figures may arise in any social grouping and such people assume positions of authority over others on the basis of personal qualities of leadership perceived in that individual by other group members. Traditional authority involves acceptance of rules that symbolize ritual or ancient practice such as religion. By contrast, Weber also focused on the power of modern bureaucracies, such as civil service, whose formal rules of procedure are legitimized by legal rational authority. Max Weber is seen as one of the most influential of social theorists in history. His analysis is complex and the historical detail that he presents to document his case is impressive, but his various snapshots taken together reveal an obviously dominant theme. Weber's further argument about power is captured by the word rationalization. We can say that rationalization is the process by which rational action becomes predominant in the social action of individuals and rationality becomes predominant in the patterns of action which are institutionalised in groups, organizations, and other collectivities. Weber was particularly interested in the rise of instrumentally rational action among individuals and formal rationality in organizations in the modern west.

A major question which occupied the latter part of Weber's scholarly career was as follows: 'why did modernization initially occur in the West and not in Eastern civilisations?' For example, why did modern science originate in the West? Why did a rational legal system first develop in Roman civilisation? Why did modern capitalism arise in the West? How to explain the Western political formation of constitutional government, the rule of law, parliamentary bodies, civil rights, and political parties?

Weber found his answer in the process of rationalization. Weber found that substantive rationality was trans-civilisational and epoch-transcending - that is, it was found in all places and at all times. However, *instrumental rationality* arose *only* in the West, providing the foundation for industriali-zation of the economy, democracy in politics, and experimental methods in science, among other distinctive features of the modern West.

When we talk about the spirit of capitalism, science and technology, rational-legal authority, and bureaucracy, we are talking about instrumentally rational action as institutionalised in the formal rationality of modern social organisations.

Weber's account of modernity, which he sees as a progressive extension of this principle of instrumental rationality, which sees action as deriving its sole meaning and interest from its results, to dominate all contemporary society. This rationalisation of social life involves an ever-greater development of technical means and a progressive relegation of the ends towards which these means are supposed to lead. An example may make this clearer. Weber argues, in *The Protestant Ethic and the Spirit of Capitalism*, that Calvinist religion represented a rationalisation of human behaviour, which focussed people's constant attention on the relationship between their everyday activity and their hope of salvation. All behaviour was scrutinised to see whether or not it represented a waste of time, and thus possibly an indication that one was not destined for salvation. This obsession with making the most of each minute, with the rationalisation of everyday life, particularly economic life, gradually came to take complete precedence over the intended goal, of demonstrating to oneself that one was likely to be destined for salvation = work hard now and reap rewards of happiness in heaven.

Weber's analysis of the development of bureaucracy is similar. Bureaucracy, for Weber, is simply the most technically efficient means of rationalisation. This means that increasingly bureaucracy takes on a life and a logic of its own which may engender an 'iron cage of rationality' (rules/routines/regulations) from which there is no escape. Think about prisons, schools, and residential care for example.

Max Weber held a view where humans are seen as pursuing a variety of ends, not always in a rational manner. The most important of these ends is the power to affect decisions of authorities. Norms and values are internalised to the extent that authorities have legitimacy. Legitimacy can be obtained by personal charisma: "Claiming special knowledge and demanding un-questioning obedience with power and privilege. Leadership may consist of one individual or a small group of core leaders" (Powell and Moody, 2001, 4). Charismatic leadership has its dark side (ie) Hitler.

His main goal was to kill as many people as possible in the most *efficient* manner, and the result was the ultimate of dehumanisation (cf. Bauman, 1989) - the murder of millions of Jewish men, women and children. The cyanide used in the gas chambers was supplied by an old established German firm through competitive bid. Their product could do the most effective job for the least possible cost, so they got the contract. In sum, the extermination camps were models of bureaucratic efficiency using the most efficient means available at that time to accomplish the goals of the Nazi government underpinned by ideology of racism.

In addition, the central tenets of the 'project of modernity' including power and progress for which Habermas (1981) attempts to formalise as practical achievements, should be put into a dark context. As the predecessors at the Frankfurt school in 1949 saw, and as Adorno and Horkheimer and Zygmunt Bauman (1989) powerfully narrate, the Holocaust provides a devastating critique of enlightenment legacy and thought and highlights the slipping into a barbarism of Nietzschean nightmares. For example, on one level, Hitler's regime in Germany merely refined and perfected 19th century techniques of social discipline. But, on yet another level, Hitler's regime was a deliberate throwback to an archaic 'society of blood', a society of savagery and a society with a lust for domination, control and power; a society which raises further questions to the enlightenment project. Coupled with this, there have been periodic episodes of inhumanity which have ranged from genocide in Rwanda in the 1970s onwards, mass genocide and 'ethnic cleansing' in former states of Yugoslavia in Kosova in 1999. The most spectacular recent example was the terrorist attacks on 'twin towers' in New York and subsequent 'wars' in Afghanistan and Iraq.

Pluralist theories see power being held by a variety of groups in society (some of which are more powerful than others) that compete with each other. Since no one group or class is able to dominate all other groups (because of checks and balances built into a democratic system of government), a "plurality" of competing interest groups, political parties, and so forth is seen to characterize democratic societies. Elite theory involves the idea that rather than there being a simple plurality of competing groups in society, there are instead a series of competing elites – powerful groups who are able to impose their will upon the rest of society. The theory of "circulating elites" is a conservative form of theorizing associated with writers such as Mosca and Pareto (Lukes 1974). C. Wright Mills's analysis has been termed as elite theory as well, but stems from the idea that certain elite groups arose to control various institutions in society. Since some institutions were more powerful than others (an economic elite, for example, is likely to be more powerful than an educational or religious elite), it followed that the elite groups who controlled such institutions would hold the balance of power in society as a whole – they would dominate politically on the structural level of power and involve the creation of a "power elite" (which we discuss in the next chapter).

The Marxist tradition elaborated the role of cultural hegemony in ideology as a means of bolstering the power of capitalism and the nation-state. Marx sees power in terms of a conflict between economic classes. A dominant class (the bourgeoisie or 'capitalist' class) owns and controls the means of production; an industrial working class, the 'proletariat', is exploited by them. Marx's analysis of social life concentrates principally on its relationship to the exercise of power. The state can be seen either as an instrument of the ruling capitalist class, or as a complex set of systems which reflects the contra-dictions of the society it is part of. Conflict is rooted in the economic sphere where the bourgeoisie own the means of production. This is a Marxist form of theorizing that argues that power is fundamentally lodged with the owners and controllers of economic production (the bourgeoisie). Political power is seen to derive from economic ownership and, in this respect, we can identify a ruling class which not only controls the means of production, distribution, and exchange in capitalist society, but also dominates and controls the institutions of political power. There are two variations of Marxist views on power. Instrumental Marxism, associated with the work of Ralph Milliband and especially *The State in Capitalist Society* (1969), attempts to demonstrate empirically the nature of ruling class domination in society. Structuralist Marxism, associated with the work of writers such as Nicos Poulantzas, especially his *Classes in Contemporary Capitalism* (1975), and Louis Althusser, concentrates more upon the structural arrangements of capitalist society. It attempts to show how a ruling class is able to dominate the rest of society economically, politically, and ideologically without the need for its members to personally oversee the workings of the state.

Finally, Michel Foucault's analysis of power has arguably been the most influential discussion of the topic over the last 30 years. Foucault's (1977) work analyzes the link between power and knowledge. He outlines a form of covert power that works through people rather than only on them. As he puts it, "power is everywhere, not because it embraces everything, but because it comes from everywhere" (1978: 93). Foucault endeavors to offer a "microphysics" of modern power (1977: 26), an analysis that focuses not on the concentration of power in the hands of the sovereign or the state but instead on how power flows through the capillaries of the social body. For Foucault, "experts" such as medical doctors are key interventionists in societal relations and, in the management of social arrangements, pursue a daunting power to classify, with consequences for the reproduction of medical knowledge. At the same time, Foucault also recognized that power itself lacks any concrete form, occurring as a locus of struggle. Resistance through defiance defines power and hence becomes possible *through* power. Without resistance, power is absent. Foucault rejects claims that any particular group or class have a monopoly over power rather, power circulates via a myriad of social networks penetrating deep into the far corners of social life playing out its effects through the everyday interactions of autonomous individuals. Power and knowledge combine in disciplinary processes that act on the body producing the modern subject as docile, productive and willing to participate in their own management (Foucault, 1977). Through these processes, power operates to differentiate groups of people and individuals from other individuals, finally producing the components of individual subjectivity.

Foucault uses the idea of 'resistance' to describe how the effects of power may be only partially successful in specific social contexts enabling challenges to and changes in existing power relations. This occurs in a number of ways but is located with two forms of possibility. First, the re-emergence of 'popular knowledges', the historical contents of conflict and struggle that have become submerged under a veneer of functionalist coherence and order; and second 'insurrections of subjugated knowledges', knowledges disqualified as inadequate, unscientific or lacking sophistication. In both these possibilities, we can see the possibility of a range of accounts i.e. professionals alienated from practice, oppressed communities, and the disadvantaged and disenfranchised.

In this formulation, Foucault (1977) departs from many conceptualizations of power by suggesting that power in itself is 'relational'. Therefore, whilst one social actor may exercise power interacting with other individuals, we also need to be aware that all other individuals also exercise 'power' in their social relationships often expressed through 'resistance' in its dance with surveillance. The outcome is to produce a dialectical relationship between knowledge, power and action that is productive in the sense of creating particular possibilities but which also maintains a level of uncertainty and unpredictability in terms of actions, providing opportunity for the exercise of power.

However, power is also fundamental to how elites dominate in society and difficulties of resistance to this. The next chapter focuses on that issue drawing from Mills' work on Power Elites.

Chapter 3

POWER-ELITES IN CONTEMPORARY SOCIETY

As a concept, "power elite" can be defined as a small group of people who control a disproportionate amount of power, wealth, and privilege and access to decision-makers in a political system.

In a pathbreaking work, Mills (1956) claims that the US power elite consists of elite members of society characterized by consensus building and the homogenization of viewpoints. This power elite has historically dominated the three major sectors of US society: economy, government, and military. Elites circulate from one sector to another, consolidating their power as they go. Mills rejects pluralist assertions that various centers of power serve as checks and balances on one another – the power-elite model suggests that those at the top encounter no real opposition and it implies a concentration of power, wealth, and prestige in the hands of the wealthy and powerful in American society.

Mills wrote that the power elite refers to "those political, economic, and military circles, which as an intricate set of overlapping small but dominant groups share decisions having at least national consequences. Insofar as national events are decided, the power elite are those who decide them" (Mills 1956: 18).

According to Mills, the governing elite in the US draws its members from three areas: (1) the highest political leaders (including the president) and a handful of key cabinet members and close advisers; (2) major corporate owners and directors; and (3) high-ranking military officers. First, the elite occupies what Mills terms the top command posts of society. These positions give their holders enormous authority over not just governmental, but also financial, educational, social, civic, and cultural institutions. A small group is able to take fundamental actions that touch everyone. Decisions made in the boardrooms of large corporations and banks affect the rates of inflation and employment, for example. Secondly, the influence of the chief executive officers of large corporations often rivals that of the secretary of commerce. Thirdly, the military play a key role in positioning themselves to address "threats" that require resources to be mobilized, as in the case of war.

Having seen how the governing elite derives its strength, it is important to consider how this power is exercised in the political arena. What roles are played by the three parts of what Mills called the "pyramid" – the elite, the middle level, and the masses – in politics? Mills suggests that the power elite establishes the basic policy agenda in such areas as national security and economics. Of course, since it only sets the general guidelines, the middle level has plenty to do implementing them, but the public has been virtually locked out.

Its main activities – writing campaign posters, expressing opinions to pollsters, voting every two or four years – are mostly symbolic. The people do not directly affect the direction of fundamental policies. Power-elite theory, in short, claims that a single elite, not a multiplicity of competing groups, decides the life-and-death issues for the nation as a whole, leaving relatively minor matters for the middle level and almost nothing for the common person. It thus paints a dark picture. Whereas pluralists (e.g., Dahl 1961) are somewhat content with what they believe is a fair, if admittedly imperfect, system, the power-elite school decries the unequal and unjust distribution of power it finds everywhere (Lukes 1974). These "top positions" encompass the posts with the authority to run programs and activities of major political, economic, legal, educational, cultural, scientific, and civic institutions.

The presence of the power elite in the political, economic, and military bureaucracies is obvious in America's recent "War on Terror" and the Middle East crisis. The oil interests (economic) are involved with President G. W. Bush and Vice-President Cheney (political) through their past connections in that field. These interconnections make the triangle complete in inter-connecting war, business, and politicians.

One criticism of Mills' perspective on power elites is that there are many wealthy people in global society, but they are not all members of the power elite. Advantageous positions for power, prestige, and wealth include the uppermost administrative positions in the three top bureaucratic organizations: in the US, for example, the Pentagon, corporate America, and the executive branch of the US government. President Clinton had a lot of power when he was the president of the US, but as a retired president his power has been diminished. Similarly, the power of Richard Nixon eroded when he resigned as president after the Watergate affair in 1974. Indeed, the position or office holds the privilege of power, not the person. Holding these positions or offices enables the elite to gain administrative control of the main bureaucratic organizations, so they are able to maintain their own wealth, power, and privilege.

For Mills, the power elite has ensured the demise of the public as an independent force in civic affairs. Mills suggests that instead of initiating policy, or even controlling those who govern them, men and women in America have become passive spectators, cheering the heroes and booing the villains, but taking little or no direct part in the action. Individuals have become increasingly alienated and estranged from politics, as can be seen in the sharp decline in electoral participation over the last several decades. As a result, the control of their destinies has fallen into the hands of the power elite.

s of
ered
ural,
tes in
War
Trade
and the
prelude
ent, it is
n which
he major
vided by
way to a
economic
of China.
on was the
ies from the
and personal
ication from
rds (McGr
USSR, a
ther co
d co
11
he

GLOBAL POWER

ı the world has been experiencing the most formidable
several decades. A major focus has been on transnational
and lack of regulation for consumer populations in
lence, these problems require a global response by the
, not just by political leaders but also by social
ere have been a number of social scientists who
enment and its legacy have impinged upon the
and social science disciplines that have attempted
political and cultural transformations in modernity
es of globalisation in the twenty-first century are
ssing ideologies in the way that was the case with
the nation state. The world is changing at a rapid
pact of change have multiple dimensions and
eographic and cultural boundaries (Turner 2006).
nsformed the way people see themselves in the
eflexively respond to the common predicament of
vokes the formulation of contending worldviews.
comparison and confrontation of worldviews are
l conflict. In such conflict, old traditions and new
role, since they can be mobilised to provide an
's view of the world – a case in point being the
mentalist groups that combine traditionalism with
response of US/UK governments that wished to
reedom' through a 'War on Terror' against such
balised world is thus integrated but not harmo-

nious, a single place but diverse, a construct of consciousness but prone to
multiplicity and fragmentation. In that context, it is highly pertinent that
critical social science steps up to the challenge and rethinks how we 'unmask
the implications of globalization and impact on modern society.

THE POWER OF GLOBALIZATION

Globalization has become one of the central but contested concept
contemporary social science (Ritzer 2004). The term has further en
everyday commentary and analysis and features in many political, cul
and economic debates. The contemporary globalised world order origina
the international organizations and regulatory systems set up after Worl
II – including the United Nations, General Agreement on Tariffs and
(now the World Trade Organization), the International Monetary Fund,
World Bank (Smart 2007). However, the end of the Cold War was the
to the maturity of the concept of globalisation. From 1989 to the pres
possible at least to imagine a 'borderless' world (Ohmae, 1990)
people, goods, ideas, and images would flow with relative ease and
global division between East and West had gone. A world d
competing ideologies of capitalism and state socialism has given
more uncertain world in which capitalism has become the dominan
and social system, even for the communist-led People's Republi
Coinciding with these changes, a major impetus to globalisati
development and availability of digital communication technolog
late 1980s with dramatic consequences for the way economic
behaviour were conducted – this has transcended to mass commu
the Internet in the 1990s to Mobile Phones from 2000 onwa
2007). The collapse of communism in Eastern Europe and the
modernising in China, plus growth of digital technologies fu
with a global restructuring of the state, finance, production, a
associated with neo-liberalism. Coupled with this, in a post 9
has been the recent 'War on Terror' and its implications for t
the geo-political global agenda.

Since the advent of industrial capitalism as a feature o
modernity, intellectual discourse has been replete with allusi
strikingly akin to those that have garnered the attention of
globalisation (Bauman 2001). Nineteenth and twentieth
and social commentary include numerous references to an

shared awareness that experiences of distance and space are inevitably transformed by the emergence of high-speed forms of technological transportation (for example, rail and air travel) and communication (the telephone) that dramatically heighten possibilities for human interaction across existing geographical and political divides (Smart 2007). Bauman has proposed nothing less than a rewriting of human history based on what he called 'the retrospective discovery' of the centrality of spatial distance and speed of communication in the constitution of all societies (Bauman 1998: 15).

Long before the introduction of the term globalisation, the appearance of novel high-speed forms of social activity generated extensive commentary about the compression of space. Indeed, Karl Marx, in 1848 formulated the first theoretical explanation of the sense of territorial compression. In Marx's account, the imperatives of capitalist production inevitably drove the bourgeoisie to:

> Nestle everywhere, settle everywhere, and establish connections everywhere. The juggernaut of industrial capitalism constituted the most basic source of technologies resulting in the annihilation of space, helping to pave the way for intercourse in every direction, universal interdependence of nations. (Marx 1979 [1848]: 476).

Thus, Marx identified an ever-rising scope and volume of transnational relations, along with technologically orchestrated process of deepening spatio-temporal integration, as central to the very 'laws of motion' of capitalist development. All manner of factors might interrupt or constrain these tendencies.

However, because they were rooted in its core relations, private property and wage labour, they would keep 'reasserting themselves', and on an ever greater scale, so long as those relations were reproduced over time. The consequence is that globalisation as a spatial process that has facilitated the emergence of a new kind of global city based on highly specialised service economies that serve specific, particularised functions in the global economic system at the expense of former logics of organisation tied to manufacturing-based economies. To enable global markets to function effectively, they need to be underpinned by local managerial work that is concentrated in cities. Further, privatisation and deregulation during the 1980s and 1990s shifted various governance functions to the corporate world, again centralising these activities in urban spaces. In post-industrial cities there is a concentration of command functions that serve as production sites for finance and the other leading industries, and provide marketplaces where firms and governments can buy financial instruments and services. Global cities become strategic sites for the acceleration of capital and information flows, and at the same time spaces of increasing socioeconomic polarisation.

One effect of this process has been that such cities have gained in importance and power relative to nation-states. There have emerged new 'corridors' and zones around nodal cities with increasingly relative independence from surrounding areas (Davis 2007). Globalisation simultaneously brings home and exports the processes of privatisation, competition, rationalisation, and deregulation as well as the transformation of all sectors of society through technology and the flexibilisation and deregulation of employment. As a process, debate centres on the uses of globalisation as the rationale and means by which corporate capital may transnationally pursue new low wage strategies and weaken the power of labour, women, and ethnic minority populations.

But whether globalisation is imagined or real requires rigorous analysis. The next section attempts to pull together main authors, ideas and trajectories of the globalisation and illustrate it by using key examples to consolidate understanding.

THEORETICAL COMPLEXITIES OF GLOBALISATION

The theorisation of globalisation is extremely complex. Roland Robertson refers to the concept of 'global consciousness', which refers to 'the compression of the world and the intensification of consciousness of the world as a whole' (1992: 8). Through thought and action, global consciousness makes the world a single place. What it means to live in this place, and how it must be ordered, become universal questions. These questions receive different answers from individuals and societies that define their position in relation to both a system of societies and the shared properties of humankind from very different perspectives. This confrontation of worldviews means that globalisation involves 'comparative interaction of different forms of life' (1992: 27). Unlike theorists who identify globalisation with late (capitalist) modernity, Robertson sees global interdependence and consciousness preceding the advent of capitalist modernity.

However, European expansion and state formation have boosted globalisation since the seventeenth century and the contemporary shape of the world in the 19th century, when international communications, transportation, and conflict dramatically intensified relationships across societal boundaries (Mann 2006). In that period, the main reference points of fully globalised order took shape: nation-state, individual self, world-system, societies, and one humanity. These elements of the global situation became 'relativised' since national societies and individuals, in particular, must interpret their very existence as parts of a larger whole. To some extent, a common framework has guided that interpretive work; for example, states can appeal to a universal doctrine of nationalism to legitimate their particularizing claims to sovereignty and cultural distinction (Delanty and Isin 2003). But such limited common principles do not provide a basis for world order.

For Anthony Giddens (1991) the concept of time-space distantiation is central. This is a process in which locales are shaped by events far away and vice versa, while social relations are disembedded, or 'lifted out' from locales. For example, peasant households in traditional societies largely produced their own means of subsistence, a tithe was often paid in kind (goods, animals, or labour), money was of limited value, and economic exchange was local and particularistic. 'Reflexive modernisation' replaced local exchange with universal exchange of money, which simplifies otherwise impossibly complex transitions and enables the circulation of highly complex forms of information and value in increasingly abstract and symbolic forms. The exchange of money establishes social relations across time and space, which under globalisation is speeded up. Similarly, expert cultures arise as a result of the scientific revolutions, which bring an increase in technical knowledge and specialization. Specialists claim 'universal' and scientific forms of knowledge, which enable the establishment of social relations across vast expanses of time and space. Social distance is created between professionals and their clients as in the modern medical model, which is based upon the universal claims of science. As expert knowledge dominates across the globe, local perspectives become devalued and modern societies are reliant on expert systems (Beck 1992). Trust is increasingly the key to the relationship between the individual and expert systems and is the glue that holds modern societies together. But where trust is undermined, individuals experience 'ontological insecurity' and a sense of insecurity with regard to their social reality (Giddens 1991).

Ohmae's (2005) concept of a 'borderless world' epitomises enthusiasm and the belief that globalisation brings improvement in human conditions. Ohmae describes an 'invisible continent' – a moving, unbounded world in which the primary linkages are now less between nations than between regions that are able to operate effectively in a global economy without being closely networked with host regions. The invisible continent can arguably be dated to

1985 when Microsoft released its first version of Windows, CNN as a 24 hours a day new channel was launched, Cisco Systems began, the first Gateway 2000 computers were shipped, and corporations such as Sun Microsystems and Dell were starting out. Today, there has been an explosion of such corporations that affect virtually every social, economic and political relationship. Transnational corporations increasingly do not treat nation states as single entities and region states make effective points of entry into the global economy. For example, when Nestlé moved into Japan, it chose the Kansai region round Osaka and Kobe rather than Tokyo as a regional doorway (Smart 2007). This fluidity of capital is creating a borderless world in which capital moves around, chasing the best products and the highest investment returns regardless of national origin.

The Internet has changed not only the way business works but also the way people interact on a personal level – from buying and selling online to planning for retirement, managing investment and on-line bank accounts. Although, in recent times, the dark side of the Internet has revealed illegitimate ways that groups and individuals use 'hyper borderless worlds' with data espionage, data theft, credit card fraud, child pornography, extremism and terrorism - are ever more common on the internet with up to £40 billion a year made by international organised crime syndicates on the web (Huber 2004).

The Internet is a global system and decisions made on virtual 'platforms' (that are created by corporations rather than governments) determine how money moves around the globe. The emergence of 'around-the-world' 24/7 financial markets, where major cross-border financial transactions are made in cyberspace represents a familiar example of the economic face of globalisation (Schneider 2007). The definition and social construction of 'the problem' of state power is transferring from the state and its citizenry to private sector global finance. For example, Powell (2006) points to how the economic stakes and social consequences of 'ageing populations' cannot be underestimated for the upholding of power by multi-national corporations. Looking ahead, the race is on for 'Global Custody' through the socially constructed 'Ticking of the Pensions Time Bomb', as described by the *Financial Times* with Europe as a 'battleground' for the US Banks (The Bank of New York, State Street Bank, JP Morgan and Citibank) competing against the European Deutsche, BNP Paribas and HSBC for custody of the growing pensions market and the highly lucrative financial services supporting it. As further incentive to eager financial enterprises, the 'global picture' in private wealth drawn from the lucrative business of pension providing is estimated by 2007 to exceed

$13,000 billion in the USA, $10,000 billion in Europe, and $7,200 billion in Asia. In less developed countries, women especially have been among those most affected by the privatization of pensions and health care, and the burden of debt repayments to agencies such as the World Bank and the IMF (Walker and Naegelhe 1999).

David Harvey emphasises the ways in which globalisation revolutionises the qualities of space and time. As space appears to shrink to what Marshall McLuhan (1975) refers to as a 'global village' of telecommunications and ecological interdependencies and as time horizons shorten to the point where the present is all there is, so we have to learn how to cope with an over-whelming sense of *compression* of spatial and temporal worlds (Harvey 1990: 240). Time-space compression that 'annihilates' space and creates 'timeless time' is driven by flexible accumulation and new technologies, the production of signs and images, just-in-time delivery, reduced turnover times and speeding up, and both de- and re-skilling. Harvey points for support to the ephemerality of fashions, products, production techniques, speedup and vertical disintegration, financial markets and computerized trading, instan-taneity and disposability, regional competitiveness. For Harvey, flexible computer-based production in Silicon Valley or the 'Third Italy' epitomises these changes. Yet it could be argued that an exclusive focus on time-space compression would be misleading. Thrift (1994) suggests that international systems reliant upon rapid electronic communication and diffusion of data do not always result in a lessening of the importance of individual actors or localised face-to-face micro-social relations. He acknowledges that the international financial system has become, to an extent, 'disembedded from place', but emphasises that transnational financial networks generate vast amounts of data and a range of 'meanings' pertaining to the interpretation of those data. The result is that inter-personal exchanges involving individual agency to negotiate, discuss, interpret and act upon the data are still of considerable importance. Since the vast majority of human activities is still tied to a concrete geographical location, the more decisive facet of globali-sation concerns the manner in which distant events and forces impact on the local or 'glocal' situation (Tomlinson 1999: 9).

At the same time, globalisation also refers to those processes whereby geographically distant events and decisions impact to a growing degree on 'glocal' higher education (Loader 2001). For example, the insistence by powerful political leaders such as George W. Bush and Tony Blair in the Western world that the International Monetary Fund (IMF) should require that Latin and South American countries commit themselves to a particular set of economic policies might result in poorly paid teachers and researchers as well as large, understaffed lecture classes in San Paolo or Lima; the latest innovations in information technology from a computer research laboratory in India could quickly change the classroom experience of students in Tokyo.

John Urry (2005) argues that the changes associated with globalisation are so far-reaching that we should now talk of a 'theory beyond societies'. This position is informed by the alleged decline of the nation-state in a globalised world, which has led to wider questioning of the idea of 'society' as a territorially bounded entity. This in turn prepares the ground for claims to the effect that since 'society' was a core theoretical concept, the very foundations of social science discipline have likewise been undermined. The central concepts of the new socialities are space (social topologies), regions (interregional competition), networks (new social morphology), and fluids (global enterprises). Mobility is central to this thesis since globalisation is the complex movement of people, images, goods, finances, and so on that constitutes a process across regions in faster and unpredictable shapes, all with no clear point of arrival or departure.

Despite the contrasting theoretical understandings of globalisation, there is some measure of agreement that it creates new opportunities or threats. For example, globalisation offers new forms of cosmopolitanism (Delanty 2006) and economic growth (Smart 2007) but also new threats and global risks (Mythen 2007) such as ecological crises of global warming, climate change and environmental pollution; global health pandemics such as 'swine flu'; and international crime and terrorism. Globalisation may be seen as encroachment and colonisation as global corporations and technologies erode local customs and ways of life, which in turn engenders new forms of protest. Giddens has argued that the effects of globalisation must also be seen as positive and that integration into the global economy increases economic activity and raises living standards. For example, Legrain (2006) claims that in 2000 the per capita income of citizens was four times greater than that in 1950. Between 1870 and 1979, production per worker became 26 times greater in Japan and 22 times greater in Sweden. In the whole world in 2000 it was double what it was in 1962. Even more significantly, Legrain (2006) argues that those nation states isolated from the global capitalist economy have done less well than those that have engaged with it. Poor countries that are open to international trade grew over six times faster in the 1970s and 1980s than those that shut themselves off from it: 4.5 percent a year, rather than 0.7 percent.

By contrast to Legrain's (2006) idealism, it can be argued that global patterns of inequality have become increasingly polarised (Estes, Biggs and

Phillipson 2003). According to the United Nations, the richest 20 percent in the world 'own' 80 percent of the wealth; the second 20 percent own 10 percent; the third 20 percent own 6 percent; the fourth 20 percent own 3 percent; and the poorest 20 percent own only 1 percent. Throughout the world, 2.7 billion people live on less than $2 per day. These global inequalities predate globalisation, of course, but there are global processes that are maintaining a highly unequal social system (Phillipson 2005). Contradictions in global society are illustrated in other ways too. The globalisation of capital may not have driven costs down in developed countries where few workers are prepared to tolerate the conditions this new model creates. Flexible global ordering systems need not just produce flexible labour, but flexible labour in excess, because to manage the supply of labour it is necessary to have a surplus. Migrants have met this need (Miles 2004). But in the wake of hostility manifest in many developed countries, especially following threats of terrorist attack in US and Europe migrants face tightening border controls and deportation of those who are not in areas where there is a shortage of skills.

Globalisation has been the focus of extensive social movement activism and 'resistance', especially to neoliberal globalism represented by bodies such as the WTO. Glasius et al. (2002) identify the emergence of a 'global civil society' in, for example, the growth of 'parallel summits' such as the 2001 Porto Alegre meeting in Brazil attended by 11,000 people to protest against the Davos (Switzerland) World Economic Forum. These are organised through multiple networks of social actors and NGOs operating on local and international levels. There may appear to be an irony that many of the internationally organised or linked social movements use globalised forms of communication (the Internet) and operate transnationally, mobilising a global consciousness and solidarities on such issues.

The major contentious claim is that globalisation is a new form of imperialism imposing US political and economic dominance over the rest of the world (Estes, Biggs and Phillipson 2003). For example, the United States represents the most significant case of privatisation as an element in the globalisation agenda, and a glimpse of what may come to pass for the broader community of nations. Pressures for more and more privatisation mount on the US state, as exemplified by the growth of the highly profitable $1.2 Trillion dollar largely private medical industrial complex, which more than tripled in size during Ronald Reagan's two presidential terms during the 1980s alone. Indeed, the medical industrial complex, comprise nearly 15% of the American economy under the Bush Administration from 2000 - 2007 even though an alarming 16% (44 million) of US citizens are uninsured for health care. The

US federal government finances around 40% of US health care, while the state limits its own activities to supporting and complementing the market (Estes and Phillipson 2003). Multinational health enterprises are an increasingly important component of the US medical industrial complex. As early as 1990, 97 US companies reported ownership of 100 hospitals with 11,974 beds in foreign countries. Pharmaceutical firms are also major global corporate players, with the total value of exported and imported pharmaceuticals estimated in excess of $110 billion in 1998 (Phillipson and Powell 2004). Added to this:

> After three decades devoted to market rhetoric, cost containment, and stunning organizational rationalization, the net result is the complete failure of any of these efforts to stem the swelling tide of problems of access and cost. Moreover, there are alarming increases in the uninsured populations among ethnic minority groups. (Held 2000: 183)

President Obama is currently seeking to transform the provision of healthcare in the US, but the vested interests of the privatised healthcare system are seeking to limit and oppose the main thrust of his proposals, presenting these as being 'socialist' extensions of state power. Paradoxically, however, the neo-liberal ideology of globalisation further bolsters the more restrictive limitations on the role of the state with respect to its citizens. David Held and his colleagues make the point that a distinctive feature of the present period is the extent to which:

> Financial globalisation has imposed an external financial discipline on governments that has contributed to both the emergence of a more market-friendly state and a shift in the balance of power between the state and financial markets. (Held 2000: 232)

In this respect, the political agenda of advanced capitalist states reflects in part the constraints of global finance, even though the specific impact of financial globalisation will vary greatly among states. A tangible consequence is the insertion of the operatives and 'requisites' of global finance into state policy-making in ways that frame, if not dictate, the parameters of state power.

Contrary to this, Sibeon (2004) suggests that national governments do 'matter', especially regarding globalisation and its implications for governance. It is Sibeon's (2004) contention that we must recognise subnational governance in addition to transnational and policy processes. The renewed emphasis upon locale and subnational governance is reflected in work focusing on the significance of regions in the policy process. Amin and Thrift (1995), for example, have outlined a focus upon mezo-level governance/policy networks within European regions. Jenson (1995) has suggested that, in the case of Canada, regional governance can be both utilised as a way of asserting regional/ethnic autonomy (as in Quebec), or exercised reluctantly (as in New Democrat-led Ontario) where subnational governments have identified a tendency for central governments to neglect or even abdicate responsibilities for maintaining standards of national economic management.

These developments can be viewed as part of a new global process of shaping the lives of present and future generations of populations in western and non-western states. The change has been variously analysed as a move from 'organised' to 'disorganised capitalism', to a shift from 'simple' to 'reflexive modernity', and to the transformation from 'fordist' to 'post-fordist economies'. The final part of this paper looks ahead and provides some reflective thoughts for questioning the extent to which a 'global social theory' is warranted.

The Future of a Global Social Theory?

At this point in the twenty first century, an array of opportunities and challenges present themselves for the study of social theory. There is a need to develop a clearer perspective on the pressures facing social groups that impinge on 'race', class, age, gender, disability and sexuality as a result of global change. A significant issue is how globalisation and its impingement on local governance is transforming the everyday texture of day to day living. In this context, the need for a framework to respond to the challenge associated with globalisation is warranted. The key dimensions here are the changing and contested form of the nation state, citizenship and nationalism; the enhanced role of supra-national bodies; the increased power of multi-national corporations; and emergence and retrenching of social inequalities across the globe.

We argue that social theory should not merely provide 'critical questions' about dynamics of social relations, but rather, it is what one does with critical questions that is the cornerstone for critical theorising. In concluding this final chapter the book, we develop this theme by highlighting the main issue of globalisation that a situated social theory will need to focus on in reflexive theorising in looking ahead for the future.

A key aim of social theory is, first, the examination of the social construction of reality and critical debunking of such contingent realities. A central task for social theory concerns the need to examine the structural inequalities and power dynamics that perpetuate current understandings of social world. An analysis that accepts enlightenment assumptions about, for example, 'equality', fails to ask the key questions about why this state of affairs holds true for some rather than for others. A critical social theory must move beyond appearances and seek explanations that overturn conformist realities. Crucially, power relations, social processes and structures must be examined as they appear in everyday relations. Links must be made between the traditional and contemporary social theories between macro, micro and meso levels of analysis, so that the pull of social inequalities can be identified and the emotional experience and daily interpretation of them explored.

A key issue in theoretical interpretation concerns the place and nature of 'society'. The ideas of society as a bounded self-sufficient entity most associated with the recent neo-functionalism of Alexander (2004) had become taken for granted within mainstream theorising. Such a formulation assumes there is a coherent and bounded society into which social integration is attainable. This view has become prominent by a small group of western societies, especially those associated with recent *'War on Terror'* who aggressively promote nation statehood and democratic freedom (Walklate and Mythen 2007). Nevertheless, the notion of society as a sovereign entity is changing profoundly with the intensifying social forces of globalisation:

> there are exceptional levels of global interdependence, unpredictable shock waves spill out 'chaotically' from one part to the system as a whole; there are not just societies but massively powerful empires roaming around the globe; and there is a mass mobility of people, objects and dangerous human wastes. (Urry 2000:13)

This critical questioning of the modernist basis to society is a challenging one to social theory. In a sense the traditional formulation of 'society' is being challenged from global forces that impinges on new technology that transforms the experience of social relations (Whyte 2007). Indeed, in a networked world, everyday life is becoming detached from the protective nation state seen to be at the core of occidental modernity. Steering a path between Giddens's (1991) 'global optimists' and 'global pessimists', it may be suggested that a new formulation is required that recognises diverse and unequal networks in and through the way people interact throughout their lives across national, transnational and sub-cultural contexts. A major dimension of inequities impinges on debates on issues such as climate change, power of multinational corporations, and third world countries of debt repayment (Mythen 2007; Phillipson 2006). The phenomenon of globalisation has transformed debates within social theory to the extent that it has re-ordered concepts typically used by social theorists across micro-macro continuum (Bauman 1998).

Ideas associated with the idea of modernity, the state, gender, class relations, ageing and ethnicity have retained their importance but their collective and individualised meaning is different and fragmented in the context of the influence of global actors and institutions (Mythen 2007).

A contentious point is that accepting the importance of globalisation also strengthens the case for rethinking social theory through re-assertion of macro analysis. Hagestad and Dannefer (2001: 66) note that the costs of micro analysis has been significant in "hampering' our ability to address what we mean by society in the context of global economic and technological change'. Given the explanatory role of social theory, globalisation is setting major new challenges in terms of interaction between individuals, communities and nation states and the global structure within which these are constructed, contested and nested. Analysing the interpretation of daily life may be more appropriately assessed in the contexts of networks and flows characteristic of global society, these producing a loosening in those attachments which have traditionally embedded people to locative settings: for Marxists in social class and for Feminists in gendered configurations. With globalisation, these attachments are maintained but recontextualised and re-embedded with the influence of transnational communities, corporations and international governmental organisations producing new agendas and challenges for how we understand 'modern society' (Turner 2006). Further, the nature of 'citizenship' and 'rights' so heavily influenced by Enlightenment philosophy are both heavily contested under the lead of the complex and commanding influences of powerful non-democratic intergovernmental structures such as the World Bank and International Monatory Fund (IMF), private multinational corporations such as banks and western states that are under new pressures associated with accelerating demography and migration. This contrasts sharply with the Enlightenment period which saw rights arguably independently defined and negotiated through various manifestations of British, European and American nation building and sovereign state-based power.

It may also be suggested that democratic rights have become more fragmented as well as individualised. What has changed is the duty and necessity to cope with these risks that are being increasingly transferred to families (Bauman 2000). The new social construction of everyday life may be defined as a global problem and issue but the social reconstruction of how experience globalisation is being cast as a personal rather than a collective responsibility. This development also implies an important role for social theory in interconnecting macro and micro perspectives with new approaches in order to understand how global processes contribute to the reshaping of the institutions in which the experiences of social groups are embedded.

A further task must be to construct new social theories about the nature of individualisation in light of more fluid borders surrounding nation states. Important questions concern whether and how people, socially differentiated, are facilitated or constrained by the spread of mobile communities along with more varied forms of belonging and citizenship. Social theory will be profoundly influenced by the 'development of a common consciousness of human society on a world scale and an increased awareness of the totality of human social relations as the largest constitutive framework of all relations' (Shaw 2002:12).

A further issue concerns the extent to which social theory may challenge the dominant institutions that reproduce and perpetuate social divisions in society. Applications of the policy sciences take for granted existing systems of capitalism as scholars work largely within 'definitions of the situation' that are framed by classical economic theories, assumptions and models of cost-effectiveness and individual level outcomes. The end result is that only a limited array of potentially viable policy options assuring the serious consideration of only incremental changes that will do little to alter the underlying structural economic problems facing social groups such as, for example, older people (Powell 2006).

In challenging this, there is a need for theorising that examines the structural forces and social processes that profoundly shape individual and group experience in the global community of the first, second and third worlds. Theoretical development from a critical perspective seeks to illuminate alternative understandings and a vision to 'what is possible'. It is a requisite to lifting the ideological veil of scientific objectivity that obscures and mystifies inequality and social injustice in a society and economy that prioritises the production of goods and services primarily for its economic and exchange value rather than for its social value and capacity to meet human needs across the world.

Chapter 5

THE PROBLEM OF POWER
AND COMMUNICATIVE ACTION

The theoretical-philosophical work of Jurgen Habermas occupies a significant position in western social and political discourse. Roderick (1986) claims Habermas represents the most important attempt at re-constructing critical theory out of the shadows of Marx. Coupled with this, Habermas uses Kant and Hegel to revitalise Marxism by developing an emancipatory theory of society. In addition, according to Delanty (2000) his relation to Adorno, Horkheimer, Benjamin and Marcuse at Frankfurt school is important in interpreting his modernist insights. Despite this, Delanty (2000) claims Habermas is more affirmative and keen towards the classical philosophical tradition particularly the 'enlightenment'. For the past two decades in particular, Habermas has written on the enlightenment project in a reflexive manner: facing up to enlightenment thought and legacy via a systematic critical analysis of the present: its historiography, pathologies, and futurology. At the same time, there has been a huge escalation of neo-Nietzschean philosophers under the labels of 'postmodernist' and 'post-structuralist' who have castigated the enlightenment to the dustbin of the history of ideas, that its metanarratives of 'progress' and 'freedom' have failed and that western rationality is exhausted (Delanty, 2000).

Habermas (1992) claims that neo-Nietzschean critiques of enlightenment fail because they lose a sense of direction. In regard to Foucault (1977), Habermas (1992) accuses him of 'cryptonormativity' and 'irrationality': the former applies because Foucault cannot explain the standards Habermas thinks must be pre-supposed in any condemnation of the present; the latter because of the appellation of Nietzsche's influence. The somewhat legendary albeit brief dispute between Habermas and Foucault turns on whether Foucault is understood to be criticising modernity from a pre-modern or postmodern view. Habermas is willing to defend his own reconstruction of the modern enlightenment tradition, against those critics of modernity of whom he considers to be anti-modern because of the reactionary implications of their views. As Habermas points out:

> 'The Young Conservatives recapitulate the basic experience of aesthetic modernity' (1981, 7).

The main assumption for Habermas (1992) is that the project of modernity can be redeemed. The diagnoses of Horkheimer, Adorno, Nietzsche, Heiddeger, Foucault and Derrida are false. Habermas's task is to strengthen the 'project of modernity' by reconstructing it vis-à-vis the 'theory of communication'. Hence, the massive task is to overcome the pessimism of late modernity, the indulgence of his predecessors at Frankurt, Adorno and Horkheimer (1949), by resolving the dilemmas of subject-centred reason in the paradigm of communicative action.

The next section highlights the significance of communicative action to the manifestation of everyday existence in modern society.

'BUILDING BLOCK' OF MODERNISM: COMMUNICATIVE ACTION

The theory of communication attempts to facilitate a continuity of language fused into the project of modernity. According to Rasmussen (1990), Ferdinand De Saussure's (1959) distinction between diachronic and synchronic is fundamental in unravelling Habermas' thought: diachronic historical-evolutionary schemes for understanding language follows the model of the enlightenment. From this perspective, Habermas' attempt to reconstitute the project of modernity through language is consistent with diachronic model of understanding language.

Language is the vehicle for the most fundamental form of social action, namely his theory of communicative action. Habermas (1981, 44) defines communicative action as:

'... that form of social interaction in which the plans of action of different actors are co-ordinated through an exchange of communicative acts, that is, through a use of language orientated towards reaching understanding'.

Sociologically, Habermas (1981) fuses micro and macro dimensions: he uses Mead and Durkheim as a theoretical bridge to develop communicative action. While Mead is important because of symbolically mediated interaction, Durkheim is important because of his analysis of the 'sacred' and process of secularization of religion. Therefore, Habermas (1981 and 1992) sees the 'language – communication' framework as a new way of retrieving the project of modernity. Habermas wants to show how the transformation from traditional society to modernity involved a progressively secularization of normatively behaviour reconstructed through communicative action. Drawing on his assessment of communicative competence of social actors, Habermas (1981) distinguishes between 'action orientated to success' and 'action orientated to understanding' and between the social and non-social contexts of action. Action orientated to success is measured via rules of rational choice; action orientated to understanding takes place through 'communicative action'. This manifestation of communicative action materialises by mutual and co-operative achievement of understanding amongst collective participants.

Communicative action is linked to the reason embodied by universal pragmatics, since it is directed by search for intersubjective recognition of validity claims (truth, rightness and sincerity) although this may be only implicitly present in any case of actual social interaction. Communicative action is based on an analysis of the social use of language oriented to reaching understanding which focuses on the action co-ordinating effects of the validity claims offered in speech acts (Habermas, 1981). Communicative action is internally linked to communicative rationality which is a central plank for a critical theory. This involves an attempt to characterise universal features of communication in their structure and consolidation that remains open to empirical rationality and verification. Similarly, Roderick (1986) interprets communicative rationality as an attempt to identify empirically the historical development of rationality structures as well as problematizing further rationality to more modern spheres of social life.

Habermas' (1981) notion of Lebenswelt or 'lifeworld' must be introduced as a contextual marker to link action theory with rationalisation processes. This means understanding not just how particular actions may be judged as rational but how rationality potential in modernity embed particular actions and makes possible rational conduct of everyday life. Habermas conceptualises the 'lifeworld' as the taken for granted universe of everyday existence. For Habermas (1981) the lifeworld is the saturation of communicative action by tradition and routinized way of doing acts. The lifeworld is a pre-interpreted set of forms of life within which daily conduct materialises.

In Habermas' view the context for the process of evolutionary development of society, culture and individual personality is the articulation of the lifeworld that correlates with an internal system of language. We can see therefore that the lifeworld forms the linguistic context for processes of communication. For Habermas (1981) through the rationalization of the lifeworld social change is said to occur. Processes of rationalization within the lifeworld are said to occur through communicative action while irrational processes of change occur through strategic action. By extending Max Weber's theory of rationalisation, Habermas claims society can flourish along lines of progressive differentiation and rationalisation. Habermas (1981), forever the eclectic theorist, draws on notions from Talcott Parsons of 'social system' to signify as it becomes more differentiated, the lifeworld becomes ever more rationalised. The important point is that as the lifeworld and social system become ever more differentiated from each other but as they do each new system developed can further life possibilities (Kellner, 1989). The non-realisation of these possibilities leads to counter-emancipation: the taking over of communicative imperatives by strategic imperatives via colonisation of the lifeworld.

'IN THE BLUE AND RED CORNERS': LYOTARD V HABERMAS

Shortly after the publication of Habermas' 'theory of communicative action', a debate on postmodernism emerged in western social theory. The debate was instigated by Derrida, Baudrillard and Lyotard on the tradition of the modern and calls for breaks within this tradition. For Lyotard (1984), Habermas' project of modernity has become obsolete and society had entered the 'postmodern condition'. Lyotard (1984) claims modernity could not think itself, get hold of itself intellectually, with distancing itself historically achieved implementations. For Lyotard (1984, 111):

'My argument is that the modern project [of realising universality] has not been abandoned or forgotten but destroyed, liquidated'.
Further, Lyotard (1984) is scathing of how Habermas will:

'... use the term 'modern' to designate any science that legitimates itself with reference to a metadiscourse making an explicit appeal to some grand narrative, such as the dialectics of the Spirit, the hermeneutics of meaning, the emancipation of the rational'.

The very concept of 'postmodernism' is defined by Lyotard (1984, 55) as 'incredulous towards metanarratives' and asks 'where after the metanarratives can legitimacy reside'. For Lyotard (1984) what Habermas is offering one more metanarrative of 'communicative action' which is a generalist and abstractual narrative of emancipation. Lyotard (1984) is against the language games of metaphysics and philosophy of science. Lyotard (1984) calls for an 'irreducible plurality' of language games each with its own 'local' rules, legitimations and practices. Postmodernism offers to move beyond Habermas' modernist narratives and is rapidly gaining currency throughout social and human science disciplines way into the 21st century (Powell, 2001). There are several themes that are shared in postmodern analysis, which consolidate Lyotard's (1984) interpretation.

First, there is distrust in the concept of absolute and objective truth. 'Truth' is viewed as contextual, situational, and conditional (Biggs and Powell, 2001). Second, emphasis is placed on fragmentation rather than universalism, again pushing away from the general and encompassing toward the particular (Powell, 2001). Third, local power is preferred over the centralized power of the nation state, and the decentralization, or the process of democratization of power, is a pervasive theme of postmodern narratives (Mestrovic, 1994). Fourth, reality is simulated but is otherwise not a very meaningful concept; reality conceived as a general and universal truth is profoundly doubted (Foucault, 1977). Fifth, we are seeing the rise and consolidation of consumer culture that tends to put 'power' in the hands of the consumers, but can also equally manipulate consumers through marketing ploys and interpolating discourses of consumer freedom by dictating costs in global market place (Biggs and Powell, 2001). Finally, diversity and difference is emphasized and valued above commonality based on homogeneity (Powell, 2001). Postmodern analysis of culture is no longer a fringe perspective as it promotes strategies of individualism and diversity; and it is critical of strategies that devalue individuals because of any characteristic that control access to knowledge, and that assault identity (Biggs and Powell, 2001). It sees ethics as situational.

The response to the conceptual development of postmodernism has infuriated as many scholars as it has intoxicated. It is no surprise to see Habermas' reaction in particular as very antagonistic of and to postmodernism. For him, either individuals encounter a strategic choice either:

'hold fast to the intentions of the Enlightenment or give up the project of modernity as lost' (Habermas, 1984, 35)

Habermas (1984, 34) defends the 'project of modernity' from the theoretical schisms of Lyotardian postmodernism which omits:

'a modernity at variance with itself of its rational content and its perspective on the future' (Habermas, 1984, 36).

Habermas (1984) in 'Philosophical Discourses of Modernity' recognised that theories of postmodernism had their roots in irrational precursory influences such as Heidegger and Nietzsche. Habermas (1984) contends that modernity 'rebels' against tradition and has valorised highly charged aesthetic experiences of novelty, dynamism, singularity and intense presence. With increase innovation in technology and science, modernity embedded a sense of foundationalism and ontological security to society and the self in general. Further, Habermas claims that the project of modernity was 'unfinished' and contained unlimited capacity for emancipatory potential. Such potential draws on the specialization of culture for the enrichment of daily life and simultaneously the rational organisational of everyday life and experience. The project of modernity has unlimited potential to increase social rationality, justice and morality; this can be realised by cognitive progression and moral boundaries of rationality. From Habermas' (1984) point of view the defence of the enlightenment is qualified. He gives sweeping castigation to the 'young conservatives' whom he accuses of setting up 'false programs of the negation of culture' which fail to realise positive contribution to project of modernity.

PUTTING HABERMAS UNDER
THE THEORETICAL MICROSCOPE

Habermas' (1981, 1984, and 1992) exhaustive, complex, and defensive theoretical arguments are very much open to scrutiny. Habermas' theoretical archrival Nikolas Luhmann (1982) has dismissively claimed:

'... there are far too many grounds and arguments... when it has not been very precisely determined in advance what is relevant and what is not ... communication can, in actual fact, not lead to anything' (Luhmann quoted in Brand, 1990, 120).

In addition, Doorne (1985 cited in Brand, 1990) claims that Habermas does not really distinguish between two contexts of analysis: firstly, formal universal pragmatics; secondly, empirical research. Similarly, Brand (1990) rejects Habermas' position because of his hostility to empirical research and deduced logic. Coupled with this, Therborn (1986 cited in Roderick, 1986, 2-3) has castigated Habermas for deviating from 'the path of true science' by developing a 'speculative' epistemology which rejects key Neo-Marxian concepts.

Ironically, there are two modernistic yet sociological grounds that Habermas fails to incorporate or appreciate in his analysis: gender and racial inequality. The former because Habermas' theorizing is built on a conception of the world in which, albeit essentialist characteristics but realities, 'middle class' 'white' 'males' dominate. The whole 'project of modernity' and associated discourses of rationality and progress have historically sided with men over women (Stanley and Pateman, 1991). The enlightenment philoso-phizing was a language based seeing women in an inferior position to that of a man; a period of patriarchal domination. Whilst Stanley and Pateman (1991) do acknowledge that Habermas' notion of emancipation is influential to feminists seeking a normative theory of consciousness and liberation, she does reserve judgement on Habermas' theory of communicative action. They see it as gender blind and perpetuates enlightenment tradition of*malestreaming* mainstream analysis of reconstituting project of modernity.

Secondly, to compound the adverse androcentric effects of 'project of modernity', it can be coupled with an accusation of eurocentricism. According to Gilroy (1992) European culture was heterogeneous during and after the enlightenment. He claims social theory can no longer understand and interpret the project of the enlightenment without understanding the periphery. For example, the legacies of slavery, colonialism and imperialism serves as reminders to the over-ambitiousness of Habermas's hopes and aspirations for social life.

In addition, the central tenets of the 'project of modernity' including rationality and progress for which Habermas (1981) attempts to formalise as practical achievements, should be put into a dark context. As the predecessors at Frankfurt school in 1949 saw, Adorno and Horkheimer and Zygmunt Bauman (1989) powerfully narrates, the Holocaust provides a devastating critique of enlightenment legacy and thought and highlights the slipping into a barbarism of Nietzchean nightmares. For example, on one level, Hitler's regime in Germany merely refined and perfected 19th century techniques of social discipline. But, on yet another level, Hitler's regime was a deliberate throwback to an archaic 'society of blood', a society of savagery and a society with a lust for domination, control and power; a society which raises further questions to the enlightenment project. Coupled with this, there have been periodic episodes of inhumanity which have ranged from genocide in Rwanda in the 1970s onwards, mass genocide and 'ethnic cleansing' in former states of Yugoslavia in Kosova in 1999 as one stark example. The most spectacular recent example was the terrorist attacks on 'twin towers' in New York and subsequent 'war' in Afghanistan. It is very difficult to implement Habermas' (1984) universalized narratives of communicative action, with so many differences between states, cultures and ideologies. It seems it is very difficult to provide a modern solution to a postmodern problem: for example, *diversity* of fundamentalist beliefs and consequent actions (postmodern), *communicative action* is very brittle in overcoming instabilities of such beliefs (Habermas' modernism).

In conclusion, Habermas' work is a concern with rethinking the tradition of critical theory and German social philosophy. Rationality, freedom and justice are not just theoretical issues to be explored and debated, but for Habermas (1981) they are practical tasks that demand commitment and achievement. Habermas' entire work seems to defend and continue the enlightenment project against the challenge of Weber (instrumental rationality), Horkheimer and Adorno and Nietzscheanism in the form of post-structuralism (Foucault and Derrida) and postmodernism (Lyotard).

Chapter 6

THE SOCIAL SHAPING OF EMOTION

INTRODUCTION

This chapter revisits and rethinks C. Wright Mills' (1959) pathbreaking work *'The Sociological Imagination'* by critical analysis of the under-theorised theme in Sociology: that of 'emotion' that is plugged into what Mills refers to as 'private troubles' and 'public issues'. The 'sociological imagination' is the ability to look at the everyday world and understand how it operates in order to make sense of people's lives. Mills (1959) claims that it is a 'state of mind', which enables social analysts to think critically about and understand the society in which they live, and place in that world as individuals and as a whole. Mills' (1959) understanding of the sociological imagination is 'a quest for sociological understanding' involving 'a form of consciousness for understanding social processes (1959, 76). It is a pathway for a person to look at their life as a result of their interaction with society. The sociological imagination requires an engagement to the study of an individual's biography but to place that biography in the wider social context of the history and tradition of the society in which an individual lives. Mills suggests that a useful way of understanding this 'imagination' is to use the 'fruitful distinction' between on the one hand 'the personal troubles of milieu' and on the other, 'the public issues of social structure'. (Mills 1959: 14). For Mills the all too common misperception on the part of many individuals is that they perceive their own biographies as just personal and private. Far too often there is a failure to see their own biographies as being interwoven and interrelated to the wider public and political 'stage' of society. Thus an 'emotion' is a 'private trouble', however for Mills the individual needs to recognise that it is one not unconnected with wider social forces of 'public issues'.

Emotions play a central role in the inter-relationship between private troubles and public issues. Emotion can be defined generally as appraisals of situational stimuli, indicating changes in physiological sensation (Timiras, 2001). They are also social constructions and individual improvisations (Hochschild, 1979) that confirm or disconfirm role-identities in sociality and culture (Layder, 2004). Typical (Heise 1987) or characteristic (MacKinnon, 2005) emotions correspond directly with the affective quality of a particular role identity and individual biography.

Typical emotions are linked to role identities through their common affective representation and quality. In this way, the private emotional lives of people are a function of the confirmation of their identity-situated selves in social interaction. The 'private issue' of an expression of emotions through displays or verbal accounts enable others to make inferences about a person's emotional experiences, and, hence, the identity a person is trying to confirm in a present situation (Jenkins, 2005). On the other hand, the 'public issue' expression of emotion is normatively regulated too. Indeed, in 1997 when Princess Diana died the media suggested that British population were 'weepers' and 'traumatised' that she had died (Layder, 2004). The media played a key role in defining the emotionality expression of 'public issues' through normativity.

The following discussion attempts to problematize emotions through some of the theoretical themes that are situated within wider social theory. In particular, we look at three broad approaches: rationality, emotionalism and social structure (that includes Durkheim, Marx, Freud, Weber, critical theory and feminism); social interactionism (that includes some of the influential themes drawn from Garfinkel, Goffman and Mead); and (social construc-tionism that includes Foucault, Bourdieu and Baudrillard). The beauty of the 'sociological imagination' is in its epistemological flexibility to accommodate both micro/macro debates about the construction of biographies and relationship to history of the present. Emotion is a key vehicle that can be used to shed light on its epistemological gaze and ontological understanding. Is emotion regulated through structure? How relevant is micro analysis to it explanation? Can we articulate discourse, embodiment and hyper-reality as conceptual tools to illuminate its complexity? The answers to these questions illustrate the relationship between micro levels of interaction amongst people (personal troubles) and structures (public issues). We also raise questions as to whether the fine line between private troubles/public issues can be transcended through exploration of post-structuralist insights. We begin our discussion with emphasis on how emotion is theorised by interactionist approaches.

INTERACTIONISM, SYMBOLISM AND SITUATIONAL RELATIONS: EMOTIONS AS PRIVATE TROUBLES

Social interactionists approach the interpenetration of emotions and social phenomena by understanding that emotions are both constructed and determined. The interactionist model points to a certain paradox; a *feeling* is what happens to us in terms of private troubles. Yet it is also what we do to make it happen. (Goffman, 1959) Emotions erupt during social interaction. Then they are judged for suitability according to cultural and ideological standards, and managed to effect culturally acceptable displays that yield social accord. Employing a symbolic interactionist perspective, emotion can be conceptualised in a number of ways. Foremost, emotion can be considered more than merely a biological act of procreation or pleasure or pain (Gane, 2005). It is a complex social interaction between two or more people. It is the dynamic interaction not only between one's own personal values, attitudes, personality dispositions, cognitions, wants, desires, and behaviours, but, more importantly, the interaction between these entities and those of others (Layder, 2004). For example, sexual behaviours, including acts of 'courtship' can be interpreted not simply as means to ends, but as acts invested with meanings that are interpreted differently by different people (Layder, 2004). Under the terrain of symbolic interactionism, such meanings and interactions could be seen as changing in a number of ways, and as able to significantly influence the negotiations that occur between sexual partners, especially depending on the degree of correspondence that results between two or more partners' attitudes, desires, behaviours, and so forth (Smith, 1998).

Both G. H. Mead and Goffman propose that people construct and understand social action so as to have important symbolic meanings affirmed by impressions generated in manifest behaviour. People credit themselves and others with specific identities during social encounters. They then engage in physical and mental work so that events create impressions that maintain sentiments attached to their identities, as well as to other categories of action (i.e., behaviours, settings, and personal conditions emotions included). Emotions are momentary personal states that reflect how events affect people. The emotion depends on the current impression of the person, and on how that impression compares to the sentiment attached to the person's identity. For example, a person might feel overwhelmed or anxious if made to seem bad and weak, but a more extreme response feeling ashamed, desperate, or depressed is to be expected if the person has a particularly good and powerful 'role' in a particular social grouping or setting. We may wish to ask what happens to the emotions in the context of social interaction? Freund (1998) argues that individuals try to regulate their feelings to fit in with the norms of the situation, and that if there are conflicting demands upon us, people may feel 'dramaturgical stress'. So people may feel 'sad' or 'happy' because a particular social situation requires that we act in one way (being cheerful and outgoing, for example) while inside people may feel a different way (such as cautious or reserved). Put together, these two oppositional motivations can leave people feeling ambivalent, ontologically insecure (cf. Giddens, 1991) and uncertain (Layder, 2004), as well as ill-equipped to deal with the situation, and this in turn leads to greater self consciousness. Perhaps individuals are engaged in this careful monitoring of their own feelings and behaviour, and it is simply that some are more successful than others at hiding their uncertainty. Hochschild (1983, 87) claims that 'we all believe that everyone else knows and understands the 'rules' governing social interaction, even though nobody ever talks about them explicitly, and so we might be forgiven for thinking that we 'ought' to disguise our ignorance with a show of confidence'. This emotion work (Hochschild 1983) forms part of everyday lives, both in the private world of the self and in the public spheres of interaction where individuals learn socially appropriate ways of acting and expression management. Hochschild referred to these codes as 'feeling rules' and argued that they were historically and culturally specific; in contemporary Western societies, the emotions had become commercialised and were often found to be 'sold' in the form of marketable services.

Thoits' (1990) typology of emotion management techniques includes implementation of new events and reinterpretation of past events as ways of managing emotions through reconstruction of the situations that evoke the emotions. Thoits notes that emotions also can be managed directly by manipulating accompanying physiology (as with drugs), by performing or fantasising expressive gestures for desired emotions, or by re-categorising one's affective sensations in terms of a desired emotion.

The personal and the normative systems unite when group members are deeply committed to their group identities; in that case, people spontaneously emote and act according to group norms in order to experience affirmation of self through the reflected appraisals of others (Burke and Reitzes, 1991). The two systems diverge when a person maintains multiple definitions of a situation simultaneously, and the actor's deepest commitment is to an identity other than the public identity. In that case, emotion management is required to prevent the display of emotions appropriate to the private identity, and to authenticate one's supposed commitment to the public identity as a public issue.

STRUCTURE, RATIONALITY AND GENDER: EMOTIONS AS 'PUBLIC ISSUES'

Social structural approaches assess the interpenetration of emotions and sociocultural phenomena by understanding that emotions emerge from the operative social structure in a situation, and emotions allow people to sense that structure, as well as the social consequences of actions. Moreover, because displays of emotion broadcast a person's subjective appraisals to others, emotions contribute tacitly to sharing views about social structure and to synchronization of rational action and feeling within a group.

Durkheim (1912/1954) proposed that rituals hold society together by producing sacred objects and moral constraints, and Collins (1990) expanded on Durkheim's theme by proposing that a common emotional mood generated in rituals creates social solidarity and diffuses charismatic emotional energies that preserve and disseminate normative group patterns. Profaning a symbol usually will elicit anger and conflict between groups or between group factions, but reaffirming symbols generates positive emotion and synchronization within the group. Durkheim (1897) would hold that the inherent emotionality of even commonplace interaction rituals is the glue that holds society together such as religion.

Conversely, Karl Marx (1843) saw society in terms of a conflict between economic classes that creating alienation. A dominant class (the bourgeoisie or 'capitalist' class) owns and controls the means of production; an industrial working class, the 'proletariat', is exploited by them. The state can be seen either as an instrument of the ruling capitalist class, or as a complex set of systems which reflects the contradictions of the society it is part of. Marx (1843) claimed that revolution was 'natural' because of the oppression of the working class. For Durkheim (1895) for members of modern society who did not feel part of the collective conscience could be led to anomie, a state of normlessness. For Marx to prevent alienation is to unite against capitalists. For

Durkheim workers should unite but with capitalists in creating consensual society. Although they did not explicitly speak about emotion, both Durkheim and Marx saw the problem of modernity was a recognition of alienation and normlessness that impinges on the regulation of individual behaviour.

Rationality was a major concern of Sigmund Freud. Freud was struck by the way that people could be more or less rational most of the time, but that they, on occasion, behave in very irrational ways. For Freud, this was very much to do with the tensions between, on the one hand culture, and on the other, instinct. For Freud the condition of humankind is in part a product of the fact that we live in a modern 'civilised' world. That is, Freud believed that 'civilization' was a modern phenomenon, and involved the development of control over individual emotions. A Freudian viewpoint would see the emotional contents of the unconscious are not easily available to consciousness because they have been repress well out of reach of our awareness because they are painful and in some sense dangerous. This unconscious is dynamic - it contains memories, perceptions, fantasies, impulses, conflicts that must be pushed back or repress in order to make life less conflictual. For Freud, this defence strategy would be un-costly for most people but for some people it leads to the development of 'neuroses'. As Julia Kristeva (1999, p327) argues:

> 'Freudian theory is more than a theory of dualism, it is a theory of contradiction and struggle'.

Following Freud, Lacan developed a concept of 'desire' that originated of processes of emotional identification with significant others and then became encoded within systems of symbolic representation, as an infant, for example, became inducted into the world of language and discourse. At the point when a child is able to speak and think as 'I' he or she is cut off from all of the flows of his/her emotional experience. Lacan (1992) presents a stark choice; the price to be paid is that for social power to be gained by entry into the world of language is having to submit to the rules of operation of the symbolic order and hence to lose touch with much of one's previous experience of desiring. This perspective can be seen as maintaining the absolutist of the rationality /emotionality dualism. One of the most important things we can draw from Freud here is again an argument about the notion of rationality and relationship to emotion. Freud paints a picture of rationality as a social construction. It could not exist without the regulating effects of society. In contrast, our inner impulses and emotional compulsions are basically irrational. All human behavioural problems occur because of this tension between the individual's irrational impulse and society's rational rules.

We can say that rationalisation is the process by which rational action becomes predominant in the social action of individuals and rationality becomes predominant in the patterns of action which are institutionalised in groups, organizations, and other collectivities. Max Weber (1883) was particularly interested in the rise of instrumentally rational action among individuals and formal rationality in organizations that crushed any form of human emotionalism in western modernity.

Weber (1883) found that substantive rationality was trans-civilisational and epoch-transcending - that is, it was found in all places and at all times. However, *instrumental rationality* arose *only* in the West, providing the foundation for industrialization of the economy, democracy in politics, and experimental methods in science, among other distinctive features of the modern West. When we talk about the spirit of capitalism, science and technology, rational-legal authority, and bureaucracy, we are talking about instrumentally rational action as institutionalised in the formal rationality of modern social organisations.

Weber's (1883) account of modernity, which he sees as a progressive extension of this principle of instrumental rationality, which sees action as deriving its sole meaning and interest from its results, to dominate all contemporary society. This rationalisation of social life involves an ever-greater development of technical means and a progressive relegation of the ends towards which these means are supposed to lead. An example may make this clearer. Weber argues, in *The Protestant Ethic and the Spirit of Capitalism*, that Calvinist religion represented a rationalisation of human behaviour, which focussed people's constant attention on the relationship between their everyday activity and their hope of salvation. All behaviour was scrutinised to see whether or not it represented a waste of time, and thus possibly an indication that one was not destined for salvation. This obsession with making the most of each minute, with the rationalisation of everyday life, particularly economic life, gradually came to take complete precedence over the intended goal, of demonstrating to oneself that one was likely to be destined for salvation equates with working hard now and reap future emotional rewards of post-physical happiness in heaven.

Weber's analysis of the development of bureaucracy is similar. Bureaucracy, for Weber, is simply the most technically efficient means of rationalisation. This means that increasingly bureaucracy takes on a life and a logic of its own which may engender an 'iron cage of rationality' (rules

/routines/regulations) from which there is no escape. Weber (1883) held a view where humans are seen as pursuing a variety of ends, not always in a rational manner. The most important of these ends is the power to affect decisions of authorities. Norms and values are internalised to the extent that authorities have legitimacy. Legitimacy can be obtained by personal charisma: "Claiming special knowledge and demanding unquestioning obedience with power and privilege. Leadership may consist of one individual or a small group of core leaders" (Powell and Moody, 2001, 4). Charismatic leadership has its dark side (ie) Hitler. The goal was to kill as many people as possible in the most *efficient* manner, and the result was the ultimate of dehumanisation (cf. Bauman, 1989) - the murder of millions of Jewish men, women and children. The cyanide used in the gas chambers was supplied by an old established German firm through competitive bid (Mestrovic, 1997). Their product could do the most effective job for the least possible cost, so they got the contract. In sum, the extermination camps were models of bureaucratic efficiency using the most efficient means available at that time to accomplish the goals of the Nazi government underpinned by ideology of racism.

Similarly, Adorno and Horkheimer sought other strategies for a critical theory of modern society relevant to understanding the positioning and detachment of emotions. Horkheimer and Adorno (1949) book *Dialectic of Enlightenment* believed that reason had been instrumentalised (see Weber's influence) and incorporated into the very structure of society. Thus reason was being used to strengthen rather than transform the system. Enlightenment had turned into its opposite and turned from being an instrument of liberation to domination. Enlightenment had always been infused with myth, according to Horkheimer and Adorno, and the project of dominating nature, of using reason to control and dominate the world, was being applied to humans in oppressive and monstrous ways. The Nazi rationalisation of death in the concentration camps and the rationalization of war during World War II raised deep questions concerning the progressive force of reason and the efficacy of immanent critique in the light of such powerful social systems. This takes a view of what Mestrovic (1997) labels as 'post-emotionalism' whereby rational means are the only manner to objectify human behaviour.

The 'McDonaldization' thesis is a very popular formulation in social theory influenced by Weber with three characteristics (Ritzer, 2004) - *efficiency* means choice of efficient means to achieve specified ends (includes assembly-line philosophy of Macs, drive-throughs, making the customer work to assemble own burgers and dispose of waste), *calculability* of process and product (quantification of meals, portion, times), *predictability* (standardised meals and Mcworkers all over the world - trained by the Hamburger University) , non-human technology - factory farms, microwaves, computerisation eg cash tills, drinks dispensers - and robot workers) (Ritzer, 2004; Ryan and Ritzer, 2007 forthcoming).

Clearly, what is efficient for the company is not necessarily so efficient for us. The downside of the organisation and its alleged negative effects - cruelty to animals, harmful components, poor health safety, worker tedium and exploitation. Ritzer has gone on to suggest there are possible ways in which rationalisation will triumph. Ritzer takes the case of Japan and *hyperrationality* - a fusion occurs between rationality of companies and what people want in life. Ritzer (2004) cites the examples of Fast food and its growth, the credit card; and Disney, shopping malls, package tours, convergences in 'McWorld' equate with virtual tourism. Emotion becomes detached from any connection with the experience of real emotions and has been Mcdonalized able to be synthesised within theme parks and heritage centres.

For Feminists, playing out the dichotomy of modernity in terms of rationality and emotion may also be seen in the public/private split that constructed the family, for example, as an oasis of emotionality, 'a haven in a harsh world' (Watson, 2001). In this picture, emotions are seen as central to the rationalisation of family life whereby women are situated, discursively and economically in positions where they may be given a 'duty' to care emotionally for others – children, older relatives and men. However, as Marshall and Witz (2004) points out this emotion bargain may actually be more complex than it appears. Women and men may enter 'partnerships' on an unequal basis in terms of material relations and this can serve to reinforce gendered inequalities in emotional relations:

> 'Women have been put in a position of being economically dependent within patriarchy but the relationship between economic dependency and emotional dependency is not straightforward. Although this is not usually made explicit within the relationship, mens dependency needs are most often met within marriage and their emotional worries by their wives. No equivalent place exists for women' (Eichenbaum and Orbach, 1985, 86-7).

Thus womens unequal social position may place them in the contradictory position of feeling dependent on men but actually being depended on by men for the servicing of *their* emotional needs.

In the context of eurocentricity of emotions, Franz Fanon (1986) analysed the emotional alienation of black people within racist and colonial social orders, being given little choice but to taker on and live within a white worldview whilst being inferiorised within it.

Discourse, Embodiment and Hyper-Reality: Emotions as Bifurcated Private Trouble/Public Issue Dualisms

A social constructionist literature on emotions has been steeped in the Cartesian tradition which treats emotions as an awkward mix of physical /physiological processes, on the one hand, and personal experiences on the other, with the bulk of attention given over to the analysis of the latter. More recently, social constructionist theory has more plausibly tried to minimize the experiential element in emotion and emphasis the construction of the social setting and role that discourses play in constructing truth games impinging on the social construction of emotions.

Within early modernity, emotions could be interpreted as 'romance', 'sentiment', or spiritualism. In late modernity, emotions have become commodified that may be consumed, induced or traded within an, to mis-paraphrase C.W Mills, 'emotional industrial complex':

> 'From psychiatrists to Agony Aunts, psychotherapists to GPs, social workers to self help manuals, we are increasingly advised or cajoled on how to manage our emotions, resolve our troubles and make the most of our lives, thereby achieving full potential'(Williams, 2001, 10).

Foucault's (1965, 1977, 1978) approach the interpenetration of emotions and sociocultural phenomena by understanding the expression of emotions as personal conduct, contrived according to power and discourses so as to effect desired interpersonal outcomes.

In this perspective, displays of emotion are not uncivilized eruptions coming from deep within individual psyches, but rather amount to sophisticated social discourse that is employed to influence others (Foucault, 1977; Kristeva, 1984; Lutz, 1997). Discourses are a set of statements, labels and assumptions that operate to 'pin' "true" definitions on what is or what is not the case. For example, the power of psychiatry in defining "mental illness". The power to label an individual as "mad", "psychotic", "anxious", "phobic", "schizophrenic" and "neurotic" (Powell, 2005) - the process of pinning such discourses to people reveals a complete lack of power from being defined as "mentally ill".

Foucault (1973) has further argued persuasively that the birth of the medical profession brought with it a different way of seeing illness and well-being related to structural and personal spaces. Most notably, the sick other became an object to be modified (Powell and Biggs, 2004). Under the 'medical gaze', people become their bodies, bodies disaggregated into a series of dysfunctional parts. This is useful for the scientific analysis of function and remedy but severely limits any perspective that takes into account inter-personal and wider social factors. Although, Heise (1989) presented an alternative approach to these issues. Moreover, because emotion displays in everyday social affairs articulate underlying ideologies that some people want legitimated, sophisticated expressions of emotion have turned into a form of labour that individuals market in capitalist societies (Hochschild, 1990)

Bourdieu's interpretation of emotions rests on the assumption that there is a continuous process of embodiment, whereby individuals are constantly opened to and in relation with the world in order to strive, cope, and carry on with life's daily emotional contingencies. According to Bourdieu, social agents's experiences of embodiment differ, because they are in a way situated in a different place in the world (Bourdieu, 2000). One can easily see such differences when one considers gender, social class, sexuality, ethnicity or age. This approach is best illustrated through Bourdieu's space of social positions, where each social position – which in his case is often defined by economic and cultural capital – is associated with a distinctive view-of-the-world that regulates emotional spaces (Bourdieu, 1984; 1998). It is through the embodied practices of everyday life that social agents are in a relation to the world, that they give meaning to it and that they comprehend it (Bourdieu, 2000). The habitus provides such a practical understanding through the action of practical sense, a notion that refers to the unconscious adjustment of social agents's practices to the constraints and opportunities imposed or offered by their emotions (Bourdieu, 1990).

The emotional body for him is an individuals way of being-in-the-world: 'the body is in the world but the social world is in the body' (Bourdieu, 2000, p.152). It is as much a social construction, where social structures are internalised, as the site of experience, desire and creativity. Similarly to Merleau-Ponty's phenomenological bodily schema, which showed how the body adapts to its environment through a system of sensory and motor relations (Detrez, 2002), Bourdieu contends that 'we learn bodily'. Often unconsciously, the body becomes attuned to the world by being exposed to its regularities (Bourdieu, 2000). As emotional individuals, we have the built-in capacity of being opened to the world and of being modified by it. This is exemplified in *Distinction* (1984), where Bourdieu focused on the body of social classes (Bourdieu, 1984) and in *Masculine Domination* (2001), where he applied his approach to the 'gendered body'. These studies have shown that distinctive bodily forms are reproduced by agent's practices, which themselves are the product of the internalisation of social spaces. The body, for Bourdieu a core entity for the reproduction of power relations and social order.

For postmodernists such as Baudrillard in the postmodern media-laden condition, we experience something called "the death of the real": we live our emotions in the realm of hyperreality that is simulated, connecting more and more deeply to things like television sitcoms, music videos, virtual reality games, or Disneyland, things that merely simulate reality.

In his book *On Seduction*, he traces *social construction of love*. He suggests that seduction is artificial and symbolic, involves flirtations, double entendres, sly looks, and whispered promises. It involves the manipulation of signs like makeup, fashion, perfumes/after shaves and gestures to achieve control over a symbolic order. On top of each of these modes is now layered the "cool" seduction of media images disseminated by television, radio and film. In his work *Cool Memories*, Baudrillard has re-claimed that the Gulf War I did not happen – only a representation of reality of what the media told us that happened; that reality is *simulation* (he points to TV programmes with canned laughter and on cue applause to suggest to viewer when to laugh and when not to). Baudrillard argues that in a postmodern culture dominated by TV, films, news media, and the Internet, the whole idea of a true or a false copy of something has been destroyed: all we have now are *simulations* of reality, which aren't any more or less "real" than the reality they simulate.

In western culture, claims Baudrillard, we take 'maps' of reality like television, film, etc. as more real than our actual lives - these "simulacra" (hyperreal copies) precede our lives. Our television "friends" (e.g. sit-com characters) might seem more alive to us than their flesh-and-blood equivalents ("did you see what Frasier did last night?"). According to Baudrillard individuals communicate by e-mail, and relate to video game characters better than friends and family. Charles Lemert makes the point that individuals drive on freeways to shopping malls full of identical chain stores and products, watch television shows about film directors and actors, go to films about television production, vote for ex-Hollywood actors for president (Lemert, 2006) – the death of the emotional social. In fact, individuals get nervous and edgy if they are away too long from computers, e-mail accounts, or texting on mobile phones (Wahidin, Powell and Zinn, 2006).

In response to the criticisms of the project of modernity made by postmodernists, Habermas wishes to consolidate the 'project of modernity' and further argues that we should not completely abandon the possibility of a rational pursuit of truth and happiness of which emotion is shaped (Steuerman, 1992, 107). He defends modernity and argues that what is needed is more philosophical discussion, not less (Steuerman, 1992, 113). Habermas states that through the use of communicative action, language and rational dialogue, the Enlightenment aims of truth, justice and freedom are still attainable alongside social consensus (Powell and Moody, 2004).

BRINGING EMOTION BACK INTO SOCIAL THEORY: A NEW SOCIOLOGICAL IMAGINATION?

It has only been comparatively recently that emotions have become the focus of sociological analysis, and this is largely because they have been seen as an individual, private affair. Yet if we are to see emotion as having at least an human relational component, we need to consider to what extent this is socially shaped in the dialectical relationship between human behaviour and social structure. Bendelow and Williams (1998) argue that there is a need to 'bring emotions back in' to social theory in a more concrete way, as they have always been present implicitly in the work of previous theorists. Williams (2000) believes that emotions have a 'deep sociality' in that they are embedded in and constitutive of social interactions, and following Bourdieu (1984) he suggests that possessing the right sort of 'emotional capital' can help us to distinguish between different groups in society. Thus if a person appears to be highly anxious, tense and embarrassed around others, we might interpret their emotional state as being shy, and this can have significant implications for our reactions to them, in terms of social inclusion or exclusion.

Furthermore, we can see the emotions as being *embodied:* we do not simply have feelings that are 'all in the mind', but rather we express our emotions through bodily signs and 'symptoms', which in the case of existential characteristics such as being shy or embarrassed, for example, might include blushing, shaking, gaze aversion. As Denzin (1984) argues, emotions are "temporarily embodied, situated self-feelings" (1984: 49) which are highly dependent on our perceptions of others and their (imagined) perceptions of us.

Emotional practices can therefore be seen as *social acts* which are significant in revealing the complex interrelationships between the individual and society via the body.

This is reflected in the culture of late modernity, in which talk *about* emotions is almost as important as the emotions themselves; Mestrovic (1997) claims that we are living in a 'postemotional society'. Lupton (1998) further argues that these discourses about emotion are extremely powerful in shaping our understandings of what certain emotions are, and may be nothing more than linguistic categories used to differentiate between different social groups.

Emotions in this sense may have no meaning outside of the words used to describe them, and so it is more important to look at the social practices from which these labels emerge. This relates very clearly to the Mills' (1959) 'sociological imagination', for it shifts the focus of our attention away from the idea of individual, private worlds of emotion to the wider context of social relations and the way in which language is used with power to identify and stigmatise certain 'types' of people or subject positions. Themes in the epistemological excursion of revisiting C. Wright Mill's (!959) *sociological imagination* and emotions are inextricably linked to 'private troubles' (micro/agency/individualised) and 'public issues' (macro/systemic/structural) in both classic and contemporary social theories: in Weber's concerns for power, legitimation, status, charisma, tradition and rationality; in Durkheim's theory of social solidarity, moral force, and symbolism; in Marx's analysis of power, consciousness to class alienation; in Mead on taking the role of the other and on the internalization of the generalized other in constituting the individual mind and small scale interactions of power.

REFERENCES

Althusser, L. (1971), "Ideology and the ideological state apparatuses", in Althusser, L. (Ed.), *Lenin and Philosophy and Other Essays*, New Left Books, London.

Baudrillard, J. (2005), *The Intelligence of Evil or the Lucidity Pact*, Palgrave, New York, NY.

Bauman, Z (1989) *Modernity and the Holocaust*, Cambridge: Polity.

Bauman, Z. (1989), *Modernity and the Holocaust*, Polity, Cambridge.

Bauman, Z. (1998), *Globalization: The Human Consequences*, Polity Press, Cambridge.

Beck, U. (1992), *Risk Society: Towards a New Modernity*, Sage, London.

Bernstein, R (1985) (Ed.) *Habermas and Modernity*, Cambridge: Polity.

Biggs, S and Powell, J.L (2001) 'A Foucauldian analysis of old age and the power of social welfare', *Journal of Aging and Social Policy* Vol.12, (2), 93-111.

Bocock, R. (1976), *Freud and Modern Society*, Van Nostrand Reinhold, Wokingham.

Boden, S. and Williams, S. (2002), "Consumption and emotion: the romantic ethic revisited", *Sociology*, Vol. 36 No. 3, pp. 493-512.

Borja, J. and Castells, M. (1997), *Local and Global: Management of Cities in the Information Age*, Earthscan, London.

Bourdieu, P. (1994), *Distinction*, Polity Press, Bristol.

Bourdieu, P. (2001), *Masculine Domination*, Polity Press, London.

Brand, A (1990) *The Force of Reason*, London: Allen Unwin.

Brenner, W.H (1989) *Elements in Modern Philosophy*, London: Prentice Hall.

Butler, J. (1998), "Merely cultural", *New Left Review,* Vol. 227, pp. 33-4.

Carey, G. and Wolfensohn, J. (1999), Creditors of the Poor - Yes, All of Us, Comment and Analysis *The Guardian*, June 15th.

Coffey, W.J. (1996), The 'newer' international division of labour, in Daniels, P.W. and Lever, W.F. (eds), *The Global Economy in Transition*, Addison Wesley Longman, Harlow, Essex.

Cook, I.G. (1997), *Contextualising Steel: Changing Locational Factors in the Steel Industry*, International Symposium on Steel Industry Development and Management, Baoshan, May.

Cook, I.G. (1999), Pressures of Globalisation, Can These Be Managed?, *Proceedings of the World Management Conference*, Beijing.

Cook, I.G. (2000a), Urban and Regional Pressures of Development, Chapter 2 in Cannon, T. (ed.), *China: Resources, Development, Environment*, Macmillan, London, in press.

Cook, I.G. (2000b), *Interpreting A Multiplicity of Regions: Globalisation, Regionalisation and Pacific Asia*, submitted paper.

Cook, I.G. and Murray, G. (2000), *China's Third Revolution: Tensions in the Transition to a Post-Communist China*, Curzon, London.

Cook, I.G. and Wang, Y. (1998), Foreign direct investment in China: patterns, processes, prospects, Chapter 6 in Cook, I.G., Doel, M.A., Li, R.Y.F. and Wang, Y. (eds), *Dynamic Asia: Business, Trade and Economic Development in Pacific Asia*, Ashgate, Aldershot, 177-208.

Dawkins, W. (1997), 'Sense of Unease Over a Britain Out in the Cold: Toyota Does Not Speak For All But There is Vague Concern in Japan', *Financial Times*, January 31st.

Dean, M. (1994), *Governmentality*, Oxford University Press, Buckingham, Oxford.

Delanty, G (2000) *Social Science*, London: Routledge.

Delanty, G. and Isin E. (eds) (2003) *Handbook of Historical Sociology*, London: Sage.

Denny, C. and Elliott, L. (1999), Fears of Big Talk But Little Money, *The Guardian*, June 14th, 11.

Dicken, P. (1993), 'The Growth Economies of Pacific Asia in Their Changing Global Context', Chapter Two in Dixon, C. and Drakakis-Smith (eds), *Economic and Social Development in Pacific Asia*, Routledge, London., 22-42.

Dicken, P. (1998), *Global Shift: Transforming the World Economy*, Third Edition, Paul Chapman, London.

Dummer, T.J.B. and Cook, I.G. (2008), Health in China and India: A Cross-Country Comparison in a Context of Rapid Globalisation, *Social Science and Medicine*, 67, 590-605.

Durkheim (1896).

Durkheim, E. (1964), in Simpson, G. (Ed.) *The Division of Labour in Society*, Free Press, New York, NY (originally published in 1893).

Elias, N. (1991), *The Symbol Theory*, Sage, London.

Estes, C.L., Biggs, S. and Phillipson, C. (2003), *Social Theory, Social Policy and Ageing: A Critical Introduction*, Maidenhead: Open University.

Fanon, F. (1986), *Black Skin, White Masks*, Pluto Press, London.

Finance and Development (1992), Recent Trends in FDI for the Developing World, 29, 50-51.

Fleming, P. (2005), *"Metaphors of resistance"*, *Management Communication Quarterly*, Vol. 19 No. 1, pp. 45-66.

Foucault, M (1977) *Discipline and Punish*, London: Tavistok.

Foucault, M. (1965), *Madness and Civilisation*, Tavistock, London.

Foucault, M. (1977), *Discipline and Punish*, Tavistock, London.

Foucault,M(1973), *The Order of Things,* Tavistock, London.

Furedi, F. (2002), *Culture of Fear: Risk Taking and the Morality of Low Expectation,* Continuum, London.

Furedi, F. (2004), *Therapy Culture: Cultivating Vulnerability in an Uncertain Age,* Routledge, London.

Gamel, C., Hengeveld, M.W., Davis, B. and Van De Tweel, I. (1995), ''Factors that influence the provision of sexual health care by Dutch cancer nurses'', *International Journal of Nursing Studies*, Vol. 32 No. 3, 301-14.

Gane, M (1981) *Baudrillard*, London: Routledge.

Giddens, A. (1998), *The Third Way: The Renewal of Social Democracy*, Polity Press, Cambridge.

Gifford, S. (1994), *Japan Among the Powers 1890-1990*, Yale University Press, New Haven and London.

Gilroy, P (1992) *Black Atlantic*, London: Hutchinson.

Goffman, E. (1959), *Presentation of Self in Everyday Life*, Doubleday, Garden City, New York, NY.

Gramsci, A. (1971), *Selections from the Prison Notebooks*, Lawrence and Wishart, London.

Habermas, J (1981) *The Theory of Communicative Action*, London: Beacon Press.

Habermas, J (1984) *The Philosophical Discourse of Modernity*, Cambridge: Polity.

Habermas, J (1992) *Postmetaphysical Thinking*, Cambridge: Polity.

Hall, S. (1986), "Variants of liberalism", in Donald, J. and Hall, S. (Eds), *Politics and Ideology*, Open University Press, Buckingham.

Henderson, J. and Forbat, L. (2002), "Relationship-based social policy: personal and policy constructions of 'care' ", *Critical Social Policy*, Vol. 22 No. 4, pp. 669-87.

Higgins, P.C. (1988), "Introduction" in Higgins, P.C. and Johnson, J.M. (Eds), *Personal Sociology*, Praeger, New York, NY.

Hogget, P. (2000), *Emotional Life and the Politics of Welfare*, Macmillan, Basingstoke.

Horkheimer, M and Adorno, T (1949) *Dialectic of Enlightenment*, Allen Unwin.

Horkheimer, M. and Adorno, T. (1949), *The Dialectic of Enlightenment*, Cambridge University Press, Cambridge.

Horschild, A. (1983), *The Managed Heart: The Commercialization of Human Feeling*, Routledge, New York, NY.

Hutton, W. (1996), *The State We're In*, Vintage, London, Revised Edition.

Jilberto, A.E.F. and Mommen, A. (1998), 'Globalization Versus Regionalization', Chapter One in Jilberto, A.E.F. and Mommen, A. (eds) , *Regionalization and Globalization in the Modern World Economy: Perspectives on the Third World and Transitional Economies*, Routledge, London, 1-26.

Kellner, D (1989) *Critical Theory, Marxism, and Modernity*, Cambridge: Polity.

Khong, Cho-Oon (1996), Pacific Asia as a Region: the View from Business, Chapter 7 in Cook, I.G., Doel, M.A. and Li, R. (eds), *Fragmented Asia: Regional Integration and National Disintegration in Pacific Asia*, Avebury, Aldershot, 167-180.

Layder, D. (2004), *Emotion in Social Life*, Sage, London.

Layder, D. (2006), *Understanding Social Theory*, 2nd ed., Sage, London.

Leader, D. (2006), *Introducing Lacan*, Totem Books, New York, NY.

Lee, B-T and Bahrin, T.S. (1998), Wither the Borders? Towards a New Dimension of Geographical Differentiation, Chapter 1 in Lee, B-T and Bahrin, T.S. (eds), *Vanishing Borders: The New International Order of the 21st Century*, Ashgate, Aldershot, 3-13.

Lee, S. (1998), Managed or Mismanaged Trade? US-Japan Trade Relations During the Clinton Presidency, Chapter 7 in Cook, I.G., Doel, M.A., Li, R. and Wang, Y. (eds), *Dynamic Asia: Business, Trade and Economic Development in Pacific Asia*, Ashgate, Aldershot, 209-233.

Lemert, C. (2006), *Social Things,* Rowman and Littlefield, Lanham, MD.

Levin, D (1993) (Ed.) *Modernity and Hegemony of Vision*, California: University of California Press.

Liu, Fu-Kuo (1996), Industrial Development and the Impetus to Regional Economic Integration in Pacific Asia, Chapter 6 in Cook, I.G., Doel, M.A. and Li, R. (eds), *Fragmented Asia: Regional Integration and National Disintegration in Pacific Asia*, Avebury, Aldershot, 137-166.

Luhmann, N. (1989), *Ecological Communication*, Polity Press, Cambridge.

Lyotard, J-F (1984) *The Postmodern Condition*, Manchester: Manchester University Press.

Marshall, M. andWitz, A. (2004), *Engendering Social Theory*, Sage, London.

Martin, H-P and Schumann, H. (1997), *The Global Trap: Globalization and the Assault on Prosperity and Democracy*, Zed, London.

Martin, R. and Rowthorn, R. (1986) (eds), *The Geography of De-industrialisation*, Macmillan, London.

May, T. (1996), Situating Social Theory, Oxford University Press, Oxford.

McCarthy, T (1978) *The Critical Theory of Jurgen Habermas*, London: Hutchinson.

McGuigan, J. (2006), "Culture and risk", in Mythen, G. and Walklate, S. (Eds), *Beyond the Risk Society: Critical Reflections on Risk and Human Security,* Open University Press, Buckingham.

Mestrovic, J. (1997), *The Barbarian Temperament*, Routledge, London.

Mestrovic, S (1993) *The Barbarian Temperament*, London: Routledge.

Miller, T. (1993), *The Well-Tempered Self: Citizenship, Culture and the Postmodern Subject,* John Hopkins University Press, Baltimore, MD.

Mills, C.W. (1959), *The Sociological Imagination*, Penguin, Harmandsworth.

Mills, CW. (1956). *The Power Elite*, Penguin, Harmandsworth

Nsouli, S.M. (1999), A Decade of Transition: An Overview of the Achievements and Challenges, *Finance and Development*, 36, 2, 2-5.

Ohmae, K. (1990), *The Borderless World: Power and Strategy in the Interlinked Economy*, Harper Collins, London.

Ouattara, A.D. (1999), Africa: An Agenda for the 21st Century, *Finance and Development*, 36, 1, 2-5.

Postel-Vinay, K. (1996), Local Actors and International Regionalism: the Case of the Sea of Japan Zone, *The Pacific Review*, 9, 489-503.

Powell, J. (2006), *Social Theory and Aging*, Rowman and Littlefield, Lanham, MD.

Powell, J.L (2001) 'Aging and Social Theory: A Sociological Review', *Social Science Paper Publisher*, 4, 2, pp.1-13 (available on-line at sspp.net).

Powell, J.L. and Moody, H.R. (2003), "Habermas and communicative action", *Theory and Science*, Vol. 5 No. 2, pp. 1-11.

Pyle, K.B. (1996), *The Making of Modern Japan*, D.C. Heath and Co., Lexington, Mass., 2nd Edition.

Rasmussen, D (1990) *Reading Habermas*, London: Blackwell.

Ritzer, G. (2004), *The Globalization of Nothing*, Pine Forge Press, Thousand Oaks, CA.

Ritzer, G. (2005), *The McDonaldization of Society*, Pine Forge Press, Thousand Oaks, CA.

Ritzer, G. (2006), *Enchanting a Disenchanted World: Revolutionizing the Means of Consumption*, Pine Forge Press, Thousand Oaks, CA.

Robertson, D. (1997), 'Introduction: East Asian Trade and the New World Trade Order', in Robertson, D. (ed.), *East Asian Trade After the Uruguay Round*, Cambridge University Press, Cambridge, 1-17.

Roderick, R (1986) *Habermas and the Foundations of Critical Theory*, London: Macmillan

Rozman, G. (1998), Flawed regionalism: reconceptualizing Northeast Asia in the 1990s, *The Pacific Review*, 11, 1-27.

Samuelson, R.J. (1999), Spotlight: The Troubled World Economy, *Brittanica Book of the Year: Events of 1998*, Encyclopaedia Britannica, Chicago, 450.

Sibeon, R. (2005), *Rethinking Social Theory*, Sage, London.

Simmons, I.G. (1996), *Changing the Face of the Earth: Culture, Environment, History*, Blackwell, Oxford, 2nd Edition.

Soros, G. (1998), *The Crisis of Global Capitalism: Open Society Endangered*, Little, Brown and Co., London.

Stanley, L and Pateman, C (1991) *Feminist Interpretations and Political Theory*, Cambridge: Polity.

Tombs, S. and Whyte, D. (2006), "Work and risk", in Mythen, G. and Walklate, S. (Eds), *Beyond the Risk Society: Critical Reflections on Risk and Human Security,* Open University Press, Buckingham.

Weber, M. (1949), *The Methodology of the Social Sciences*, Shils, E. and Finch, H. (Eds), Free Press, Glencoe, IL.

Wong, D.H. (1961), "The oversocialized concept of man in modern sociology", *American Sociological Review*, Vol. 26, pp. 183-93.

Wong, J. (1999), *China's Dynamic Economic Growth in the Context of East Asia*, Keynote paper presented to the Chinese Economic Association (UK) Annual Conference on The Chinese Economy and Industry in the 21st Century, Middlesex Business School, London, March.

INDEX